C-1466 CAREER EXAMINATION SERIES

This is your
PASSBOOK for...

Secretary

Test Preparation Study Guide
Questions & Answers

COPYRIGHT NOTICE

This book is SOLELY intended for, is sold ONLY to, and its use is RESTRICTED to individual, bona fide applicants or candidates who qualify by virtue of having seriously filed applications for appropriate license, certificate, professional and/or promotional advancement, higher school matriculation, scholarship, or other legitimate requirements of education and/or governmental authorities.

This book is NOT intended for use, class instruction, tutoring, training, duplication, copying, reprinting, excerption, or adaptation, etc., by:

1) Other publishers
2) Proprietors and/or Instructors of "Coaching" and/or Preparatory Courses
3) Personnel and/or Training Divisions of commercial, industrial, and governmental organizations
4) Schools, colleges, or universities and/or their departments and staffs, including teachers and other personnel
5) Testing Agencies or Bureaus
6) Study groups which seek by the purchase of a single volume to copy and/or duplicate and/or adapt this material for use by the group as a whole without having purchased individual volumes for each of the members of the group
7) Et al.

Such persons would be in violation of appropriate Federal and State statutes.

PROVISION OF LICENSING AGREEMENTS – Recognized educational, commercial, industrial, and governmental institutions and organizations, and others legitimately engaged in educational pursuits, including training, testing, and measurement activities, may address request for a licensing agreement to the copyright owners, who will determine whether, and under what conditions, including fees and charges, the materials in this book may be used them. In other words, a licensing facility exists for the legitimate use of the material in this book on other than an individual basis. However, it is asseverated and affirmed here that the material in this book CANNOT be used without the receipt of the express permission of such a licensing agreement from the Publishers. Inquiries re licensing should be addressed to the company, attention rights and permissions department.

All rights reserved, including the right of reproduction in whole or in part, in any form or by any means, electronic or mechanical, including photocopying, recording, or by any information storage and retrieval system, without permission in writing from the Publisher.

Copyright © 2024 by
National Learning Corporation

212 Michael Drive, Syosset, NY 11791
(516) 921-8888 • www.passbooks.com
E-mail: info@passbooks.com

PUBLISHED IN THE UNITED STATES OF AMERICA

PASSBOOK® SERIES

THE *PASSBOOK® SERIES* has been created to prepare applicants and candidates for the ultimate academic battlefield – the examination room.

At some time in our lives, each and every one of us may be required to take an examination – for validation, matriculation, admission, qualification, registration, certification, or licensure.

Based on the assumption that every applicant or candidate has met the basic formal educational standards, has taken the required number of courses, and read the necessary texts, the *PASSBOOK® SERIES* furnishes the one special preparation which may assure passing with confidence, instead of failing with insecurity. Examination questions – together with answers – are furnished as the basic vehicle for study so that the mysteries of the examination and its compounding difficulties may be eliminated or diminished by a sure method.

This book is meant to help you pass your examination provided that you qualify and are serious in your objective.

The entire field is reviewed through the huge store of content information which is succinctly presented through a provocative and challenging approach – the question-and-answer method.

A climate of success is established by furnishing the correct answers at the end of each test.

You soon learn to recognize types of questions, forms of questions, and patterns of questioning. You may even begin to anticipate expected outcomes.

You perceive that many questions are repeated or adapted so that you can gain acute insights, which may enable you to score many sure points.

You learn how to confront new questions, or types of questions, and to attack them confidently and work out the correct answers.

You note objectives and emphases, and recognize pitfalls and dangers, so that you may make positive educational adjustments.

Moreover, you are kept fully informed in relation to new concepts, methods, practices, and directions in the field.

You discover that you are actually taking the examination all the time: you are preparing for the examination by "taking" an examination, not by reading extraneous and/or supererogatory textbooks.

In short, this PASSBOOK®, used directedly, should be an important factor in helping you to pass your test.

SECRETARY

Secretaries, under supervision, perform typing, secretarial and related office work with limited latitude for independent judgment; perform typing work including copy typing from rough or clear drafts, typing statistical tables, and typing transcription from tapes and varityping; perform secretarial work, including scheduling appointments and other general office work; perform basic word processing assignments using a personal computer, word processing equipment or other automated office equipment; may perform basic data entry functions; review and correct typed material to ensure correct spelling, syllabification, punctuation, and proper format; may respond to routine telephone calls; refer calls and visitors to appropriate staff. All Secretaries perform related work.

EXAMPLES OF WORK:
Prepares correspondence, documents, records and other written material in final or draft form using handwritten, rough drafts, marked copy, oral records or data from various equipment as the source of material;
Composes and prepares correspondence on matters where policies and procedures are well defined;
Maintains and updates database/spreadsheet records on a personal computer;
Screens callers or visitors to determine the nature of the inquiry and refers to appropriate party or office and answers inquiries as appropriate;
Establishes and maintains confidential and general office files;
Explains established program policies and procedures to the general public/clients and obtains routine information for program purposes;
Receives sorts and distributes incoming mail;
Checks, codes and processes requisitions, claims and bills;
Prepares and maintains financial, statistical and personnel records;
Monitors and tracks status of program activities;
Orders supplies and materials;
Collects and gathers information to be used as a basis for reports and memoranda and prepares summaries;
Transmits instructions from supervisor to staff and follows up to ensure deadlines are met;
Supervises subordinate clerical personnel;
Answers telephone and gives out information;
May schedule conferences, meetings and make travel arrangements;
Operates a personal computer, copier and other related peripheral office equipment.

SCOPE OF THE EXAMINATION
The multiple-choice test may include questions on English language usage; reading comprehension; number facility; alphabetical and numerical filing; clerical accuracy, including proofreading and matching; spelling; grammar, usage, punctuation; keyboarding practices; office record keeping; office practices; and other related areas.

HOW TO TAKE A TEST

I. YOU MUST PASS AN EXAMINATION

A. WHAT EVERY CANDIDATE SHOULD KNOW

Examination applicants often ask us for help in preparing for the written test. What can I study in advance? What kinds of questions will be asked? How will the test be given? How will the papers be graded?

As an applicant for a civil service examination, you may be wondering about some of these things. Our purpose here is to suggest effective methods of advance study and to describe civil service examinations.

Your chances for success on this examination can be increased if you know how to prepare. Those "pre-examination jitters" can be reduced if you know what to expect. You can even experience an adventure in good citizenship if you know why civil service exams are given.

B. WHY ARE CIVIL SERVICE EXAMINATIONS GIVEN?

Civil service examinations are important to you in two ways. As a citizen, you want public jobs filled by employees who know how to do their work. As a job seeker, you want a fair chance to compete for that job on an equal footing with other candidates. The best-known means of accomplishing this two-fold goal is the competitive examination.

Exams are widely publicized throughout the nation. They may be administered for jobs in federal, state, city, municipal, town or village governments or agencies.

Any citizen may apply, with some limitations, such as the age or residence of applicants. Your experience and education may be reviewed to see whether you meet the requirements for the particular examination. When these requirements exist, they are reasonable and applied consistently to all applicants. Thus, a competitive examination may cause you some uneasiness now, but it is your privilege and safeguard.

C. HOW ARE CIVIL SERVICE EXAMS DEVELOPED?

Examinations are carefully written by trained technicians who are specialists in the field known as "psychological measurement," in consultation with recognized authorities in the field of work that the test will cover. These experts recommend the subject matter areas or skills to be tested; only those knowledges or skills important to your success on the job are included. The most reliable books and source materials available are used as references. Together, the experts and technicians judge the difficulty level of the questions.

Test technicians know how to phrase questions so that the problem is clearly stated. Their ethics do not permit "trick" or "catch" questions. Questions may have been tried out on sample groups, or subjected to statistical analysis, to determine their usefulness.

Written tests are often used in combination with performance tests, ratings of training and experience, and oral interviews. All of these measures combine to form the best-known means of finding the right person for the right job.

II. HOW TO PASS THE WRITTEN TEST

A. NATURE OF THE EXAMINATION

To prepare intelligently for civil service examinations, you should know how they differ from school examinations you have taken. In school you were assigned certain definite pages to read or subjects to cover. The examination questions were quite detailed and usually emphasized memory. Civil service exams, on the other hand, try to discover your present ability to perform the duties of a position, plus your potentiality to learn these duties. In other words, a civil service exam attempts to predict how successful you will be. Questions cover such a broad area that they cannot be as minute and detailed as school exam questions.

In the public service similar kinds of work, or positions, are grouped together in one "class." This process is known as *position-classification*. All the positions in a class are paid according to the salary range for that class. One class title covers all of these positions, and they are all tested by the same examination.

B. FOUR BASIC STEPS

1) Study the announcement

How, then, can you know what subjects to study? Our best answer is: "Learn as much as possible about the class of positions for which you've applied." The exam will test the knowledge, skills and abilities needed to do the work.

Your most valuable source of information about the position you want is the official exam announcement. This announcement lists the training and experience qualifications. Check these standards and apply only if you come reasonably close to meeting them.

The brief description of the position in the examination announcement offers some clues to the subjects which will be tested. Think about the job itself. Review the duties in your mind. Can you perform them, or are there some in which you are rusty? Fill in the blank spots in your preparation.

Many jurisdictions preview the written test in the exam announcement by including a section called "Knowledge and Abilities Required," "Scope of the Examination," or some similar heading. Here you will find out specifically what fields will be tested.

2) Review your own background

Once you learn in general what the position is all about, and what you need to know to do the work, ask yourself which subjects you already know fairly well and which need improvement. You may wonder whether to concentrate on improving your strong areas or on building some background in your fields of weakness. When the announcement has specified "some knowledge" or "considerable knowledge," or has used adjectives like "beginning principles of…" or "advanced … methods," you can get a clue as to the number and difficulty of questions to be asked in any given field. More questions, and hence broader coverage, would be included for those subjects which are more important in the work. Now weigh your strengths and weaknesses against the job requirements and prepare accordingly.

3) Determine the level of the position

Another way to tell how intensively you should prepare is to understand the level of the job for which you are applying. Is it the entering level? In other words, is this the position in which beginners in a field of work are hired? Or is it an intermediate or advanced level? Sometimes this is indicated by such words as "Junior" or "Senior" in the class title. Other jurisdictions use Roman numerals to designate the level – Clerk I, Clerk II, for example. The word "Supervisor" sometimes appears in the title. If the level is not indicated by the title, check the description of duties. Will you be working under very close supervision, or will you have responsibility for independent decisions in this work?

4) Choose appropriate study materials

Now that you know the subjects to be examined and the relative amount of each subject to be covered, you can choose suitable study materials. For beginning level jobs, or even advanced ones, if you have a pronounced weakness in some aspect of your training, read a modern, standard textbook in that field. Be sure it is up to date and has general coverage. Such books are normally available at your library, and the librarian will be glad to help you locate one. For entry-level positions, questions of appropriate difficulty are chosen – neither highly advanced questions, nor those too simple. Such questions require careful thought but not advanced training.

If the position for which you are applying is technical or advanced, you will read more advanced, specialized material. If you are already familiar with the basic principles of your field, elementary textbooks would waste your time. Concentrate on advanced textbooks and technical periodicals. Think through the concepts and review difficult problems in your field.

These are all general sources. You can get more ideas on your own initiative, following these leads. For example, training manuals and publications of the government agency which employs workers in your field can be useful, particularly for technical and professional positions. A letter or visit to the government department involved may result in more specific study suggestions, and certainly will provide you with a more definite idea of the exact nature of the position you are seeking.

III. KINDS OF TESTS

Tests are used for purposes other than measuring knowledge and ability to perform specified duties. For some positions, it is equally important to test ability to make adjustments to new situations or to profit from training. In others, basic mental abilities not dependent on information are essential. Questions which test these things may not appear as pertinent to the duties of the position as those which test for knowledge and information. Yet they are often highly important parts of a fair examination. For very general questions, it is almost impossible to help you direct your study efforts. What we can do is to point out some of the more common of these general abilities needed in public service positions and describe some typical questions.

1) General information

Broad, general information has been found useful for predicting job success in some kinds of work. This is tested in a variety of ways, from vocabulary lists to questions about current events. Basic background in some field of work, such as sociology or economics, may be sampled in a group of questions. Often these are principles which have become familiar to most persons through exposure rather than through formal training. It is difficult to advise you how to study for these questions; being alert to the world around you is our best suggestion.

2) Verbal ability

An example of an ability needed in many positions is verbal or language ability. Verbal ability is, in brief, the ability to use and understand words. Vocabulary and grammar tests are typical measures of this ability. Reading comprehension or paragraph interpretation questions are common in many kinds of civil service tests. You are given a paragraph of written material and asked to find its central meaning.

3) Numerical ability

Number skills can be tested by the familiar arithmetic problem, by checking paired lists of numbers to see which are alike and which are different, or by interpreting charts and graphs. In the latter test, a graph may be printed in the test booklet which you are asked to use as the basis for answering questions.

4) Observation

A popular test for law-enforcement positions is the observation test. A picture is shown to you for several minutes, then taken away. Questions about the picture test your ability to observe both details and larger elements.

5) Following directions

In many positions in the public service, the employee must be able to carry out written instructions dependably and accurately. You may be given a chart with several columns, each column listing a variety of information. The questions require you to carry out directions involving the information given in the chart.

6) Skills and aptitudes

Performance tests effectively measure some manual skills and aptitudes. When the skill is one in which you are trained, such as typing or shorthand, you can practice. These tests are often very much like those given in business school or high school courses. For many of the other skills and aptitudes, however, no short-time preparation can be made. Skills and abilities natural to you or that you have developed throughout your lifetime are being tested.

Many of the general questions just described provide all the data needed to answer the questions and ask you to use your reasoning ability to find the answers. Your best preparation for these tests, as well as for tests of facts and ideas, is to be at your physical and mental best. You, no doubt, have your own methods of getting into an exam-taking mood and keeping "in shape." The next section lists some ideas on this subject.

IV. KINDS OF QUESTIONS

Only rarely is the "essay" question, which you answer in narrative form, used in civil service tests. Civil service tests are usually of the short-answer type. Full instructions for answering these questions will be given to you at the examination. But in case this is your first experience with short-answer questions and separate answer sheets, here is what you need to know:

1) **Multiple-choice Questions**

Most popular of the short-answer questions is the "multiple choice" or "best answer" question. It can be used, for example, to test for factual knowledge, ability to solve problems or judgment in meeting situations found at work.

A multiple-choice question is normally one of three types—
- It can begin with an incomplete statement followed by several possible endings. You are to find the one ending which *best* completes the statement, although some of the others may not be entirely wrong.
- It can also be a complete statement in the form of a question which is answered by choosing one of the statements listed.

- It can be in the form of a problem – again you select the best answer.

Here is an example of a multiple-choice question with a discussion which should give you some clues as to the method for choosing the right answer:

When an employee has a complaint about his assignment, the action which will *best* help him overcome his difficulty is to
- A. discuss his difficulty with his coworkers
- B. take the problem to the head of the organization
- C. take the problem to the person who gave him the assignment
- D. say nothing to anyone about his complaint

In answering this question, you should study each of the choices to find which is best. Consider choice "A" – Certainly an employee may discuss his complaint with fellow employees, but no change or improvement can result, and the complaint remains unresolved. Choice "B" is a poor choice since the head of the organization probably does not know what assignment you have been given, and taking your problem to him is known as "going over the head" of the supervisor. The supervisor, or person who made the assignment, is the person who can clarify it or correct any injustice. Choice "C" is, therefore, correct. To say nothing, as in choice "D," is unwise. Supervisors have and interest in knowing the problems employees are facing, and the employee is seeking a solution to his problem.

2) True/False Questions

The "true/false" or "right/wrong" form of question is sometimes used. Here a complete statement is given. Your job is to decide whether the statement is right or wrong.

SAMPLE: A roaming cell-phone call to a nearby city costs less than a non-roaming call to a distant city.

This statement is wrong, or false, since roaming calls are more expensive.

This is not a complete list of all possible question forms, although most of the others are variations of these common types. You will always get complete directions for answering questions. Be sure you understand *how* to mark your answers – ask questions until you do.

V. RECORDING YOUR ANSWERS

Computer terminals are used more and more today for many different kinds of exams.

For an examination with very few applicants, you may be told to record your answers in the test booklet itself. Separate answer sheets are much more common. If this separate answer sheet is to be scored by machine – and this is often the case – it is highly important that you mark your answers correctly in order to get credit.

An electronic scoring machine is often used in civil service offices because of the speed with which papers can be scored. Machine-scored answer sheets must be marked with a pencil, which will be given to you. This pencil has a high graphite content which responds to the electronic scoring machine. As a matter of fact, stray dots may register as answers, so do not let your pencil rest on the answer sheet while you are pondering the correct answer. Also, if your pencil lead breaks or is otherwise defective, ask for another.

Since the answer sheet will be dropped in a slot in the scoring machine, be careful not to bend the corners or get the paper crumpled.

The answer sheet normally has five vertical columns of numbers, with 30 numbers to a column. These numbers correspond to the question numbers in your test booklet. After each number, going across the page are four or five pairs of dotted lines. These short dotted lines have small letters or numbers above them. The first two pairs may also have a "T" or "F" above the letters. This indicates that the first two pairs only are to be used if the questions are of the true-false type. If the questions are multiple choice, disregard the "T" and "F" and pay attention only to the small letters or numbers.

Answer your questions in the manner of the sample that follows:

32. The largest city in the United States is
    A. Washington, D.C.
    B. New York City
    C. Chicago
    D. Detroit
    E. San Francisco

1) Choose the answer you think is best. (New York City is the largest, so "B" is correct.)
2) Find the row of dotted lines numbered the same as the question you are answering. (Find row number 32)
3) Find the pair of dotted lines corresponding to the answer. (Find the pair of lines under the mark "B.")
4) Make a solid black mark between the dotted lines.

VI. BEFORE THE TEST

Common sense will help you find procedures to follow to get ready for an examination. Too many of us, however, overlook these sensible measures. Indeed, nervousness and fatigue have been found to be the most serious reasons why applicants fail to do their best on civil service tests. Here is a list of reminders:

- Begin your preparation early – Don't wait until the last minute to go scurrying around for books and materials or to find out what the position is all about.
- Prepare continuously – An hour a night for a week is better than an all-night cram session. This has been definitely established. What is more, a night a week for a month will return better dividends than crowding your study into a shorter period of time.
- Locate the place of the exam – You have been sent a notice telling you when and where to report for the examination. If the location is in a different town or otherwise unfamiliar to you, it would be well to inquire the best route and learn something about the building.
- Relax the night before the test – Allow your mind to rest. Do not study at all that night. Plan some mild recreation or diversion; then go to bed early and get a good night's sleep.
- Get up early enough to make a leisurely trip to the place for the test – This way unforeseen events, traffic snarls, unfamiliar buildings, etc. will not upset you.
- Dress comfortably – A written test is not a fashion show. You will be known by number and not by name, so wear something comfortable.

- Leave excess paraphernalia at home – Shopping bags and odd bundles will get in your way. You need bring only the items mentioned in the official notice you received; usually everything you need is provided. Do not bring reference books to the exam. They will only confuse those last minutes and be taken away from you when in the test room.
- Arrive somewhat ahead of time – If because of transportation schedules you must get there very early, bring a newspaper or magazine to take your mind off yourself while waiting.
- Locate the examination room – When you have found the proper room, you will be directed to the seat or part of the room where you will sit. Sometimes you are given a sheet of instructions to read while you are waiting. Do not fill out any forms until you are told to do so; just read them and be prepared.
- Relax and prepare to listen to the instructions
- If you have any physical problem that may keep you from doing your best, be sure to tell the test administrator. If you are sick or in poor health, you really cannot do your best on the exam. You can come back and take the test some other time.

VII. AT THE TEST

The day of the test is here and you have the test booklet in your hand. The temptation to get going is very strong. Caution! There is more to success than knowing the right answers. You must know how to identify your papers and understand variations in the type of short-answer question used in this particular examination. Follow these suggestions for maximum results from your efforts:

1) Cooperate with the monitor

The test administrator has a duty to create a situation in which you can be as much at ease as possible. He will give instructions, tell you when to begin, check to see that you are marking your answer sheet correctly, and so on. He is not there to guard you, although he will see that your competitors do not take unfair advantage. He wants to help you do your best.

2) Listen to all instructions

Don't jump the gun! Wait until you understand all directions. In most civil service tests you get more time than you need to answer the questions. So don't be in a hurry. Read each word of instructions until you clearly understand the meaning. Study the examples, listen to all announcements and follow directions. Ask questions if you do not understand what to do.

3) Identify your papers

Civil service exams are usually identified by number only. You will be assigned a number; you must not put your name on your test papers. Be sure to copy your number correctly. Since more than one exam may be given, copy your exact examination title.

4) Plan your time

Unless you are told that a test is a "speed" or "rate of work" test, speed itself is usually not important. Time enough to answer all the questions will be provided, but this does not mean that you have all day. An overall time limit has been set. Divide the total time (in minutes) by the number of questions to determine the approximate time you have for each question.

5) Do not linger over difficult questions

If you come across a difficult question, mark it with a paper clip (useful to have along) and come back to it when you have been through the booklet. One caution if you do this – be sure to skip a number on your answer sheet as well. Check often to be sure that you have not lost your place and that you are marking in the row numbered the same as the question you are answering.

6) Read the questions

Be sure you know what the question asks! Many capable people are unsuccessful because they failed to *read* the questions correctly.

7) Answer all questions

Unless you have been instructed that a penalty will be deducted for incorrect answers, it is better to guess than to omit a question.

8) Speed tests

It is often better NOT to guess on speed tests. It has been found that on timed tests people are tempted to spend the last few seconds before time is called in marking answers at random – without even reading them – in the hope of picking up a few extra points. To discourage this practice, the instructions may warn you that your score will be "corrected" for guessing. That is, a penalty will be applied. The incorrect answers will be deducted from the correct ones, or some other penalty formula will be used.

9) Review your answers

If you finish before time is called, go back to the questions you guessed or omitted to give them further thought. Review other answers if you have time.

10) Return your test materials

If you are ready to leave before others have finished or time is called, take ALL your materials to the monitor and leave quietly. Never take any test material with you. The monitor can discover whose papers are not complete, and taking a test booklet may be grounds for disqualification.

VIII. EXAMINATION TECHNIQUES

1) Read the general instructions carefully. These are usually printed on the first page of the exam booklet. As a rule, these instructions refer to the timing of the examination; the fact that you should not start work until the signal and must stop work at a signal, etc. If there are any *special* instructions, such as a choice of questions to be answered, make sure that you note this instruction carefully.

2) When you are ready to start work on the examination, that is as soon as the signal has been given, read the instructions to each question booklet, underline any key words or phrases, such as *least, best, outline, describe* and the like. In this way you will tend to answer as requested rather than discover on reviewing your paper that you *listed without describing*, that you selected the *worst* choice rather than the *best* choice, etc.

3) If the examination is of the objective or multiple-choice type – that is, each question will also give a series of possible answers: A, B, C or D, and you are called upon to select the best answer and write the letter next to that answer on your answer paper – it is advisable to start answering each question in turn. There may be anywhere from 50 to 100 such questions in the three or four hours allotted and you can see how much time would be taken if you read through all the questions before beginning to answer any. Furthermore, if you come across a question or group of questions which you know would be difficult to answer, it would undoubtedly affect your handling of all the other questions.

4) If the examination is of the essay type and contains but a few questions, it is a moot point as to whether you should read all the questions before starting to answer any one. Of course, if you are given a choice – say five out of seven and the like – then it is essential to read all the questions so you can eliminate the two that are most difficult. If, however, you are asked to answer all the questions, there may be danger in trying to answer the easiest one first because you may find that you will spend too much time on it. The best technique is to answer the first question, then proceed to the second, etc.

5) Time your answers. Before the exam begins, write down the time it started, then add the time allowed for the examination and write down the time it must be completed, then divide the time available somewhat as follows:
    - If 3-1/2 hours are allowed, that would be 210 minutes. If you have 80 objective-type questions, that would be an average of 2-1/2 minutes per question. Allow yourself no more than 2 minutes per question, or a total of 160 minutes, which will permit about 50 minutes to review.
    - If for the time allotment of 210 minutes there are 7 essay questions to answer, that would average about 30 minutes a question. Give yourself only 25 minutes per question so that you have about 35 minutes to review.

6) The most important instruction is to *read each question* and make sure you know what is wanted. The second most important instruction is to *time yourself properly* so that you answer every question. The third most important instruction is to *answer every question*. Guess if you have to but include something for each question. Remember that you will receive no credit for a blank and will probably receive some credit if you write something in answer to an essay question. If you guess a letter – say "B" for a multiple-choice question – you may have guessed right. If you leave a blank as an answer to a multiple-choice question, the examiners may respect your feelings but it will not add a point to your score. Some exams may penalize you for wrong answers, so in such cases *only*, you may not want to guess unless you have some basis for your answer.

7) Suggestions
    a. Objective-type questions
        1. Examine the question booklet for proper sequence of pages and questions
        2. Read all instructions carefully
        3. Skip any question which seems too difficult; return to it after all other questions have been answered
        4. Apportion your time properly; do not spend too much time on any single question or group of questions

5. Note and underline key words – *all, most, fewest, least, best, worst, same, opposite,* etc.
6. Pay particular attention to negatives
7. Note unusual option, e.g., unduly long, short, complex, different or similar in content to the body of the question
8. Observe the use of "hedging" words – *probably, may, most likely,* etc.
9. Make sure that your answer is put next to the same number as the question
10. Do not second-guess unless you have good reason to believe the second answer is definitely more correct
11. Cross out original answer if you decide another answer is more accurate; do not erase until you are ready to hand your paper in
12. Answer all questions; guess unless instructed otherwise
13. Leave time for review

b. Essay questions
1. Read each question carefully
2. Determine exactly what is wanted. Underline key words or phrases.
3. Decide on outline or paragraph answer
4. Include many different points and elements unless asked to develop any one or two points or elements
5. Show impartiality by giving pros and cons unless directed to select one side only
6. Make and write down any assumptions you find necessary to answer the questions
7. Watch your English, grammar, punctuation and choice of words
8. Time your answers; don't crowd material

8) Answering the essay question

Most essay questions can be answered by framing the specific response around several key words or ideas. Here are a few such key words or ideas:

M's: manpower, materials, methods, money, management
P's: purpose, program, policy, plan, procedure, practice, problems, pitfalls, personnel, public relations
   a. Six basic steps in handling problems:
      1. Preliminary plan and background development
      2. Collect information, data and facts
      3. Analyze and interpret information, data and facts
      4. Analyze and develop solutions as well as make recommendations
      5. Prepare report and sell recommendations
      6. Install recommendations and follow up effectiveness

   b. Pitfalls to avoid
      1. *Taking things for granted* – A statement of the situation does not necessarily imply that each of the elements is necessarily true; for example, a complaint may be invalid and biased so that all that can be taken for granted is that a complaint has been registered

2. *Considering only one side of a situation* – Wherever possible, indicate several alternatives and then point out the reasons you selected the best one
3. *Failing to indicate follow up* – Whenever your answer indicates action on your part, make certain that you will take proper follow-up action to see how successful your recommendations, procedures or actions turn out to be
4. *Taking too long in answering any single question* – Remember to time your answers properly

IX. AFTER THE TEST

Scoring procedures differ in detail among civil service jurisdictions although the general principles are the same. Whether the papers are hand-scored or graded by machine we have described, they are nearly always graded by number. That is, the person who marks the paper knows only the number – never the name – of the applicant. Not until all the papers have been graded will they be matched with names. If other tests, such as training and experience or oral interview ratings have been given, scores will be combined. Different parts of the examination usually have different weights. For example, the written test might count 60 percent of the final grade, and a rating of training and experience 40 percent. In many jurisdictions, veterans will have a certain number of points added to their grades.

After the final grade has been determined, the names are placed in grade order and an eligible list is established. There are various methods for resolving ties between those who get the same final grade – probably the most common is to place first the name of the person whose application was received first. Job offers are made from the eligible list in the order the names appear on it. You will be notified of your grade and your rank as soon as all these computations have been made. This will be done as rapidly as possible.

People who are found to meet the requirements in the announcement are called "eligibles." Their names are put on a list of eligible candidates. An eligible's chances of getting a job depend on how high he stands on this list and how fast agencies are filling jobs from the list.

When a job is to be filled from a list of eligibles, the agency asks for the names of people on the list of eligibles for that job. When the civil service commission receives this request, it sends to the agency the names of the three people highest on this list. Or, if the job to be filled has specialized requirements, the office sends the agency the names of the top three persons who meet these requirements from the general list.

The appointing officer makes a choice from among the three people whose names were sent to him. If the selected person accepts the appointment, the names of the others are put back on the list to be considered for future openings.

That is the rule in hiring from all kinds of eligible lists, whether they are for typist, carpenter, chemist, or something else. For every vacancy, the appointing officer has his choice of any one of the top three eligibles on the list. This explains why the person whose name is on top of the list sometimes does not get an appointment when some of the persons lower on the list do. If the appointing officer chooses the second or third eligible, the No. 1 eligible does not get a job at once, but stays on the list until he is appointed or the list is terminated.

X. HOW TO PASS THE INTERVIEW TEST

The examination for which you applied requires an oral interview test. You have already taken the written test and you are now being called for the interview test – the final part of the formal examination.

You may think that it is not possible to prepare for an interview test and that there are no procedures to follow during an interview. Our purpose is to point out some things you can do in advance that will help you and some good rules to follow and pitfalls to avoid while you are being interviewed.

What is an interview supposed to test?

The written examination is designed to test the technical knowledge and competence of the candidate; the oral is designed to evaluate intangible qualities, not readily measured otherwise, and to establish a list showing the relative fitness of each candidate – as measured against his competitors – for the position sought. Scoring is not on the basis of "right" and "wrong," but on a sliding scale of values ranging from "not passable" to "outstanding." As a matter of fact, it is possible to achieve a relatively low score without a single "incorrect" answer because of evident weakness in the qualities being measured.

Occasionally, an examination may consist entirely of an oral test – either an individual or a group oral. In such cases, information is sought concerning the technical knowledges and abilities of the candidate, since there has been no written examination for this purpose. More commonly, however, an oral test is used to supplement a written examination.

Who conducts interviews?

The composition of oral boards varies among different jurisdictions. In nearly all, a representative of the personnel department serves as chairman. One of the members of the board may be a representative of the department in which the candidate would work. In some cases, "outside experts" are used, and, frequently, a businessman or some other representative of the general public is asked to serve. Labor and management or other special groups may be represented. The aim is to secure the services of experts in the appropriate field.

However the board is composed, it is a good idea (and not at all improper or unethical) to ascertain in advance of the interview who the members are and what groups they represent. When you are introduced to them, you will have some idea of their backgrounds and interests, and at least you will not stutter and stammer over their names.

What should be done before the interview?

While knowledge about the board members is useful and takes some of the surprise element out of the interview, there is other preparation which is more substantive. It *is* possible to prepare for an oral interview – in several ways:

1) Keep a copy of your application and review it carefully before the interview

This may be the only document before the oral board, and the starting point of the interview. Know what education and experience you have listed there, and the sequence and dates of all of it. Sometimes the board will ask you to review the highlights of your experience for them; you should not have to hem and haw doing it.

2) Study the class specification and the examination announcement

Usually, the oral board has one or both of these to guide them. The qualities, characteristics or knowledges required by the position sought are stated in these documents. They offer valuable clues as to the nature of the oral interview. For example, if the job involves supervisory responsibilities, the announcement will usually indicate that knowledge of modern supervisory methods and the qualifications of the candidate as a supervisor will be tested. If so, you can expect such questions, frequently in the form of a hypothetical situation which you are expected to solve. NEVER go into an oral without knowledge of the duties and responsibilities of the job you seek.

3) Think through each qualification required

Try to visualize the kind of questions you would ask if you were a board member. How well could you answer them? Try especially to appraise your own knowledge and background in each area, *measured against the job sought*, and identify any areas in which you are weak. Be critical and realistic – do not flatter yourself.

4) Do some general reading in areas in which you feel you may be weak

For example, if the job involves supervision and your past experience has NOT, some general reading in supervisory methods and practices, particularly in the field of human relations, might be useful. Do NOT study agency procedures or detailed manuals. The oral board will be testing your understanding and capacity, not your memory.

5) Get a good night's sleep and watch your general health and mental attitude

You will want a clear head at the interview. Take care of a cold or any other minor ailment, and of course, no hangovers.

What should be done on the day of the interview?

Now comes the day of the interview itself. Give yourself plenty of time to get there. Plan to arrive somewhat ahead of the scheduled time, particularly if your appointment is in the fore part of the day. If a previous candidate fails to appear, the board might be ready for you a bit early. By early afternoon an oral board is almost invariably behind schedule if there are many candidates, and you may have to wait. Take along a book or magazine to read, or your application to review, but leave any extraneous material in the waiting room when you go in for your interview. In any event, relax and compose yourself.

The matter of dress is important. The board is forming impressions about you – from your experience, your manners, your attitude, and your appearance. Give your personal appearance careful attention. Dress your best, but not your flashiest. Choose conservative, appropriate clothing, and be sure it is immaculate. This is a business interview, and your appearance should indicate that you regard it as such. Besides, being well groomed and properly dressed will help boost your confidence.

Sooner or later, someone will call your name and escort you into the interview room. *This is it.* From here on you are on your own. It is too late for any more preparation. But remember, you asked for this opportunity to prove your fitness, and you are here because your request was granted.

What happens when you go in?

The usual sequence of events will be as follows: The clerk (who is often the board stenographer) will introduce you to the chairman of the oral board, who will introduce you to the other members of the board. Acknowledge the introductions before you sit down. Do not be surprised if you find a microphone facing you or a stenotypist sitting by. Oral interviews are usually recorded in the event of an appeal or other review.

Usually the chairman of the board will open the interview by reviewing the highlights of your education and work experience from your application – primarily for the benefit of the other members of the board, as well as to get the material into the record. Do not interrupt or comment unless there is an error or significant misinterpretation; if that is the case, do not hesitate. But do not quibble about insignificant matters. Also, he will usually ask you some question about your education, experience or your present job – partly to get you to start talking and to establish the interviewing "rapport." He may start the actual questioning, or turn it over to one of the other members. Frequently, each member undertakes the questioning on a particular area, one in which he is perhaps most competent, so you can expect each member to participate in the examination. Because time is limited, you may also expect some rather abrupt switches in the direction the questioning takes, so do not be upset by it. Normally, a board member will not pursue a single line of questioning unless he discovers a particular strength or weakness.

After each member has participated, the chairman will usually ask whether any member has any further questions, then will ask you if you have anything you wish to add. Unless you are expecting this question, it may floor you. Worse, it may start you off on an extended, extemporaneous speech. The board is not usually seeking more information. The question is principally to offer you a last opportunity to present further qualifications or to indicate that you have nothing to add. So, if you feel that a significant qualification or characteristic has been overlooked, it is proper to point it out in a sentence or so. Do not compliment the board on the thoroughness of their examination – they have been sketchy, and you know it. If you wish, merely say, "No thank you, I have nothing further to add." This is a point where you can "talk yourself out" of a good impression or fail to present an important bit of information. Remember, *you close the interview yourself.*

The chairman will then say, "That is all, Mr. _____, thank you." Do not be startled; the interview is over, and quicker than you think. Thank him, gather your belongings and take your leave. Save your sigh of relief for the other side of the door.

How to put your best foot forward

Throughout this entire process, you may feel that the board individually and collectively is trying to pierce your defenses, seek out your hidden weaknesses and embarrass and confuse you. Actually, this is not true. They are obliged to make an appraisal of your qualifications for the job you are seeking, and they want to see you in your best light. Remember, they must interview all candidates and a non-cooperative candidate may become a failure in spite of their best efforts to bring out his qualifications. Here are 15 suggestions that will help you:

1) **Be natural – Keep your attitude confident, not cocky**

If you are not confident that you can do the job, do not expect the board to be. Do not apologize for your weaknesses, try to bring out your strong points. The board is interested in a positive, not negative, presentation. Cockiness will antagonize any board member and make him wonder if you are covering up a weakness by a false show of strength.

2) **Get comfortable, but don't lounge or sprawl**

Sit erectly but not stiffly. A careless posture may lead the board to conclude that you are careless in other things, or at least that you are not impressed by the importance of the occasion. Either conclusion is natural, even if incorrect. Do not fuss with your clothing, a pencil or an ashtray. Your hands may occasionally be useful to emphasize a point; do not let them become a point of distraction.

3) **Do not wisecrack or make small talk**

This is a serious situation, and your attitude should show that you consider it as such. Further, the time of the board is limited – they do not want to waste it, and neither should you.

4) Do not exaggerate your experience or abilities

In the first place, from information in the application or other interviews and sources, the board may know more about you than you think. Secondly, you probably will not get away with it. An experienced board is rather adept at spotting such a situation, so do not take the chance.

5) If you know a board member, do not make a point of it, yet do not hide it

Certainly you are not fooling him, and probably not the other members of the board. Do not try to take advantage of your acquaintanceship – it will probably do you little good.

6) Do not dominate the interview

Let the board do that. They will give you the clues – do not assume that you have to do all the talking. Realize that the board has a number of questions to ask you, and do not try to take up all the interview time by showing off your extensive knowledge of the answer to the first one.

7) Be attentive

You only have 20 minutes or so, and you should keep your attention at its sharpest throughout. When a member is addressing a problem or question to you, give him your undivided attention. Address your reply principally to him, but do not exclude the other board members.

8) Do not interrupt

A board member may be stating a problem for you to analyze. He will ask you a question when the time comes. Let him state the problem, and wait for the question.

9) Make sure you understand the question

Do not try to answer until you are sure what the question is. If it is not clear, restate it in your own words or ask the board member to clarify it for you. However, do not haggle about minor elements.

10) Reply promptly but not hastily

A common entry on oral board rating sheets is "candidate responded readily," or "candidate hesitated in replies." Respond as promptly and quickly as you can, but do not jump to a hasty, ill-considered answer.

11) Do not be peremptory in your answers

A brief answer is proper – but do not fire your answer back. That is a losing game from your point of view. The board member can probably ask questions much faster than you can answer them.

12) Do not try to create the answer you think the board member wants

He is interested in what kind of mind you have and how it works – not in playing games. Furthermore, he can usually spot this practice and will actually grade you down on it.

13) Do not switch sides in your reply merely to agree with a board member

Frequently, a member will take a contrary position merely to draw you out and to see if you are willing and able to defend your point of view. Do not start a debate, yet do not surrender a good position. If a position is worth taking, it is worth defending.

14) Do not be afraid to admit an error in judgment if you are shown to be wrong

The board knows that you are forced to reply without any opportunity for careful consideration. Your answer may be demonstrably wrong. If so, admit it and get on with the interview.

15) Do not dwell at length on your present job

The opening question may relate to your present assignment. Answer the question but do not go into an extended discussion. You are being examined for a *new* job, not your present one. As a matter of fact, try to phrase ALL your answers in terms of the job for which you are being examined.

Basis of Rating

Probably you will forget most of these "do's" and "don'ts" when you walk into the oral interview room. Even remembering them all will not ensure you a passing grade. Perhaps you did not have the qualifications in the first place. But remembering them will help you to put your best foot forward, without treading on the toes of the board members.

Rumor and popular opinion to the contrary notwithstanding, an oral board wants you to make the best appearance possible. They know you are under pressure – but they also want to see how you respond to it as a guide to what your reaction would be under the pressures of the job you seek. They will be influenced by the degree of poise you display, the personal traits you show and the manner in which you respond.

ABOUT THIS BOOK

This book contains tests divided into Examination Sections. Go through each test, answering every question in the margin. We have also attached a sample answer sheet at the back of the book that can be removed and used. At the end of each test look at the answer key and check your answers. On the ones you got wrong, look at the right answer choice and learn. Do not fill in the answers first. Do not memorize the questions and answers, but understand the answer and principles involved. On your test, the questions will likely be different from the samples. Questions are changed and new ones added. If you understand these past questions you should have success with any changes that arise. Tests may consist of several types of questions. We have additional books on each subject should more study be advisable or necessary for you. Finally, the more you study, the better prepared you will be. This book is intended to be the last thing you study before you walk into the examination room. Prior study of relevant texts is also recommended. NLC publishes some of these in our Fundamental Series. Knowledge and good sense are important factors in passing your exam. Good luck also helps. So now study this Passbook, absorb the material contained within and take that knowledge into the examination. Then do your best to pass that exam.

EXAMINATION SECTION

EXAMINATION SECTION
TEST 1

DIRECTIONS: Each question or incomplete statement is followed by several suggested answers or completions. Select the one that BEST answers the question or completes the statement. *PRINT THE LETTER OF THE CORRECT ANSWER IN THE SPACE AT THE RIGHT.*

1. If you open a personal letter by mistake, the one of the following actions which it would generally be BEST for you to take is to

    A. ignore your error, attach the envelope to the letter, and distribute in the usual manner
    B. personally give the addressee the letter without any explanation
    C. place the letter inside the envelope, indicate under your initials that it was opened in error, and give it to the addressee
    D. reseal the envelope or place the contents in another envelope and pass on to addressee

    1.____

2. If you receive a telephone call regarding a matter which your office does not handle, you should FIRST

    A. give the caller the telephone number of the proper office so that he can dial again
    B. offer to transfer the caller to the proper office
    C. suggest that the caller redial since he probably dialed incorrectly
    D. tell the caller he has reached the wrong office and then hang up

    2.____

3. When you answer the telephone, the MOST important reason for identifying yourself and your organization is to

    A. give the caller time to collect his or her thoughts
    B. impress the caller with your courtesy
    C. inform the caller that he or she has reached the right number
    D. set a business-like tone at the beginning of the conversation

    3.____

4. The one of the following cases in which you would NOT place a special notation in the left margin of a letter that you have typed is when

    A. one of the copies is intended for someone other than the addressee of the letter
    B. you enclose a flyer with the letter
    C. you sign your superior's name to the letter, at his or her request
    D. the letter refers to something being sent under separate cover

    4.____

5. Suppose that you accidentally cut a letter or enclosure as you are opening an envelope with a paper knife.
The one of the following that you should do FIRST is to

    A. determine whether the document is important
    B. clip or staple the pieces together and process as usual
    C. mend the cut document with transparent tape
    D. notify the sender that the communication was damaged and request another copy

    5.____

1

6. It is generally advisable to leave at least six inches of working space in a file drawer. This procedure is MOST useful in

   A. decreasing the number of filing errors
   B. facilitating the sorting of documents and folders
   C. maintaining a regular program of removing inactive records
   D. preventing folders and papers from being torn

7. Of the following, the MOST important reason to sort large volumes of documents before filing is that sorting

   A. decreases the need for cross-referencing
   B. eliminates the need to keep the files up to date
   C. prevents overcrowding of the file drawers
   D. saves time and energy in filing

8. When typing a preliminary draft of a report, the one of the following which you should generally NOT do is to

   A. erase typing errors and deletions rather than Xing them out
   B. leave plenty of room at the top, bottom, and sides of each page
   C. make only the number of copies that you are asked to make
   D. type double or triple space

9. The BEST way for a receptionist to deal with a situation in which she must leave her desk for a long time is to

   A. ask someone to take her place while she is away
   B. leave a note or sign on her desk which indicates the time she will return
   C. take a chance that no one will arrive while she is gone and leave her desk unattended
   D. tell a co-worker to ask any visitors that arrive to wait until she returns

10. Suppose that two individuals come up to your desk at the same time. One of them asks you for the location of the nearest public phone. After you answer the question, you turn to the second person who asks you the same question.
    The one of the following actions which it would be BEST for you to take in this situation is to

    A. ignore the second person since he obviously overheard your first answer
    B. point out that you just answered the same question and quickly repeat the information
    C. politely repeat the information to the second individual
    D. tell the second person to follow the first to the public telephone

11. The one of the following which is necessary to do when sending a document to be printed on an office printer is to

    A. close all files not being printed
    B. send the document to the correct printer
    C. print a series of test pages
    D. refresh the printer's ink supply

12. When typing names or titles on a roll of folder labels, the one of the following which it is MOST important to do is to type the caption

    A. as it appears on the papers to be placed in the folder
    B. in capital letters
    C. in exact indexing or filing order
    D. so that it appears near the bottom of the folder tab when the label is attached

13. The MOST important reason for placing a plastic or metal shield with cutouts over a small area to be erased from a sheet inserted in a typewriter is that the shield

    A. decreases the weakening of the paper fibers caused by erasure
    B. enables you to erase without smearing adjoining letters or adjacent lines
    C. prevents erasure particles from falling into the machine
    D. prevents the sheet from slipping while the erasure is being made

14. Before typing on more than one copy of a printed form, the one of the following which you should do FIRST is to

    A. align the type so that the tails of the longer letters will rest on the lines printed on the form
    B. check the alignment of the copies of the forms by holding them up to the light
    C. insert the form into the typewriter and then insert the copies of the form
    D. insert the copies of the form into the typewriter and then insert the original

15. The one of the following which it is NOT necessary to do when preparing a typewriter for paper is to

    A. clean the type
    B. disengage the typewriter ribbon
    C. move the paper bail rollers beyond the outer margins
    D. set the paper guide in the forward position

16. The process of *justifying* typewritten copy involves typing the copy so that

    A. each paragraph appears to be approximately the same size
    B. no long words are broken up at the end of a line
    C. the right and left hand margins are even
    D. there is enough room to enter proofreading marks at the end of each line

17. An *attention line* is used in correspondence to

    A. indicate to the person receiving the correspondence that it contains an enclosure
    B. direct correspondence addressed to an organization to a particular individual within the organization
    C. greet the recipient of the correspondence
    D. highlight the main concern of the correspondence

18. The MOST important reason for a person in charge of a petty cash fund to obtain receipts for payments is that this practice would tend to

    A. decrease robberies by delivery personnel
    B. eliminate the need to keep a record of petty cash expenditures

C. prove that the fund has been used properly
D. provide a record of the need for cash in the daily operations of the office

19. The one of the following which is the BEST procedure to follow when making a short insert in a completed dictation is to

    A. label the insert with a letter and indicate the position of the insert in the text by writing the identifying letter in the proper place
    B. squeeze the insert into its proper place within the main text of the dictation
    C. take down the insert and check the placement with the person who dictated when you are ready to transcribe your notes
    D. transcribe the dictation into longhand including the insert in its proper position

20. The one of the following procedures which will be MOST efficient in helping you to quickly open your dictation notebook to a clean sheet is to

    A. clip or place a rubberband around the used portion of the notebook
    B. leave the book out and open to a clean page when not in use
    C. transcribe each dictation after it is given and rip out the used pages
    D. use a book marker to indicate which portion of the notebook has been used

21. The purpose of dating your dictation notebooks is GENERALLY to

    A. enable you to easily refer to your notes at a later date
    B. insure that you transcribe your notes in the order in which they were dictated
    C. set up a precise record-keeping procedure
    D. show your employer that you pay attention to detail

22. The one of the following which it is MOST advisable to do before transcribing your dictation notes is to

    A. check the syllabification of long words for typing purposes
    B. edit your notes
    C. number the pages of dictation
    D. sort them by the kind of typing format required

23. As a secretary, the one of the following which is LEAST important in writing a letter under your own signature is

    A. the accuracy of the information
    B. the appropriateness of the language
    C. the reason for the letter
    D. your supervisor's approval of the final copy

24. In a typed letter, the reference line is used

    A. for identification purposes on typed letters of more than one page
    B. to indicate under what heading the copy of the letter should be filed
    C. to indicate who dictated the letter and who typed it
    D. to make the subject of the letter prominent, by typing it a single space below the salutation

25. A secretary is MOST likely to employ a form letter when
    A. an answer is not required
    B. the same information must be repeated from letter to letter
    C. there is not enough information to write a detailed reply
    D. varied correspondence must be sent out quickly

KEY (CORRECT ANSWERS)

1.	C	11.	B
2.	B	12.	C
3.	C	13.	B
4.	C	14.	B
5.	C	15.	D
6.	D	16.	C
7.	D	17.	B
8.	A	18.	C
9.	A	19.	A
10.	C	20.	A

21.	A
22.	B
23.	D
24.	C
25.	B

TEST 2

DIRECTIONS: Each question or incomplete statement is followed by several suggested answers or completions. Select the one that BEST answers the question or completes the statement. *PRINT THE LETTER OF THE CORRECT ANSWER IN THE SPACE AT THE RIGHT.*

Questions 1-12.

DIRECTIONS: In Questions 1 through 12, choose the lettered word which means MOST NEARLY the same as the italicized word in the sentence.

1. The aims of the students and the aims of the faculty often *coincide*. 1.____
   A. agree B. are ignored
   C. conflict D. are misinterpreted

2. The secretary of the Sociology Department was responsible for setting up an index of *relevant* magazine articles. 2.____
   A. applicable B. controversial
   C. miscellaneous D. recent

3. One of the secretary's duties consisted of sorting and filing *facsimiles* of student term papers. 3.____
   A. bibliographical listings
   B. exact copies
   C. summaries
   D. supporting documentation

4. *Stringent* requirements for advanced Physics courses often result in small class sizes. 4.____
   A. lengthy B. remarkable C. rigid D. vague

5. The professor explained that the report was too *verbose* to be submitted. 5.____
   A. brief B. specific C. general D. wordy

6. The faculty meeting *pre-empted* the conference room in the Dean's office. 6.____
   A. appropriated B. emptied
   C. filled D. reserved

7. The professor's credentials became a subject of *controversy*. 7.____
   A. annoyance B. debate C. envy D. review

8. The professor developed a different central theme during every *semester*. 8.____
   A. bi-annual period of instruction
   B. orientation period
   C. slide demonstration
   D. weekly lecture series

9. The college offered a variety of *seminars* to upperclassmen. 9.____

A. reading courses with no formal supervision
B. study courses for small groups of students engaged in research under a teacher
C. guidance conferences with grade advisors
D. work experiences in different occupational fields

10. The dean pointed out that the *focus* of the study was not clear. 10.____

    A. end   B. objective   C. follow-up   D. location

11. The faculty of the anthropology department agreed that the departmental program was *deficient*. 11.____

    A. excellent
    B. inadequate
    C. demanding
    D. sufficient

12. The secretary was asked to type a rough draft of a college course *syllabus*. 12.____

    A. directory of departments and services
    B. examination schedule
    C. outline of a course of study
    D. rules and regulations

Questions 13-20.

DIRECTIONS: Each of questions 13 through 20 consists of three sets of names and name codes. In each question, the two names and name codes on the same line are supposed to be exactly the same.

Look carefully at each set of names and codes and mark your answer

    (A) if there are mistakes in all three sets
    (B) if there are mistakes in two of the sets
    (C) if there is a mistake in only one set
    (D) if there are no mistakes in any of the sets

The following sample question is given to help you understand the procedure:

McCabe, John N. - V53162   Macade, John N. - V53162
Howard, Joan S. - J24791   Howard, Joan S. - J24791
Ware, Susan B. - A45068   Ware, Susan B. - A45968

In the above sample question, the names and name codes of the first set are not exactly the same because of the spelling of the last name (MaCabe - Macade). The names and name codes of the second set are exactly the same. The names and name codes of the third set are not exactly the same because the two name codes are different (A45068 - A45968). Since there are mistakes in only 2 of the sets, the answer to the sample question is B.

13. Powell, Michael C. - 78537F   Powell, Michael C. - 78537F   13.____
    Martinez, Pablo J - 24435P   Martinez, Pablo J. - 24435P
    MacBane, Eliot M. - 98674E   MacBane, Eliot M. - 98674E

14. Fitz-Kramer Machines Inc. - 259090 Fitz-Kramer Machines Inc. - 259090   14._____
    Marvel Cleaning Service - 482057 Marvel Cleaning Service - 482657
    Donato, Carl G. - 637418 Danato, Carl G. - 687418

15. Martin Davison Trading Corp. - 43108T Martin Davidson Trading Corp. - 43108T   15._____
    Cotwald Lighting Fixtures - 76065L Cotwald Lighting Fixtures - 70056L
    R. Crawford Plumbers - 23157C R. Crawford Plumbers - 23157G

16. Fraiman Engineering Corp. - M4773 Friaman Engineering Corp. - M4773   16._____
    Neuman, Walter B. - N7745 Neuman, Walter B. - N7745
    Pierce, Eric M. - W6304 Pierce, Eric M. - W6304

17. Constable, Eugene - B63837 Comstable, Eugene - B64837   17._____
    Derrick, Paul - H27119 Derrik, Paul - H27119
    Heller, Karen - S49606 Heller, Karen - S46906

18. Hernando Delivery Service   Hernando Delivery Service   18._____
    Co. - D7456 Co. - D7456
    Barettz Electrical Supplies - N5392 Barettz Electrical Supplies - N5392
    Tanner, Abraham - M4798 Tanner, Abraham - M4798

19. Kalin Associates - R38641 Kaline Associates - R38641   19._____
    Sealey, Robert E. - P63533 Sealey, Robert E. - P63553
    Sealsi Office Furniture - R36742 Scalsi Office Furniture - R36742

20. Janowsky, Philip M. - 742213 Janowsky, Philip M. - 742213   20._____
    Hansen, Thomas H. - 934816 Hanson, Thomas H. - 934816
    L. Lester and Son Inc. - 294568 L. Lester and Son Inc. - 294568

Questions 21-28.

DIRECTIONS: Each question 21 through 28 consists of four names. For each question, choose the one of the four names that should be LAST if the four names were arranged in alphabetical order in accordance with the RULES FOR ALPHABETICAL FILING given below. Read these rules carefully. Then, for each question, indicate in the correspondingly numbered space at the right the letter before the name that should be LAST in alphabetical order.

RULES FOR ALPHABETICAL FILING

Names of Individuals

1. The names of individuals are filed in strict alphabetical order, first according to last name, then according to first name or initial, and finally according to middle name or initial. For example: George Allen comes before Edward Bell, and Leonard P. Reston comes before Lucille B. Reston.

2. When last names are the same, for example, A. Green and Agnes Green, the one with the initials comes before the one with the name written out when the first initials are identical.

3. When first and last names are alike, the name without a middle initial comes before the one with a middle name or initial. For example: John Doe comes before both John A. Doe and John Alan Doe.

4. When first and last names are the same, the name with a middle initial comes before the one with a middle name beginning with the same initial. For example: Jack R. Hertz comes before Jack Richard Hertz.

5. Prefixes such as De, O', Mac, Mc, and Van are filed as written and are treated as part of the names they come before. For example: Robert O'Dea is filed before David Olsen.

6. Abbreviated names are treated as if they were spelled out. For example: Chas. is filed as Charles and Thos. is filed as Thomas.

7. Titles and designations such as Dr., Mr., and Prof, are disregarded in filing,

Names of Business Organizations

1. The names of business organizations are filed according to the order in which each word in the name appears. When an organization name bears the name of a person, it is filed according to the rules for filing names of people as given above. For example: William Smith Service Co. comes before Television Distributors, Inc.

2. When the following words are part of a business name, they are disregarded: the, of, and.

3. When there are numbers in a name, they are treated as if they were spelled out. For example: 10th Street Bootery is filed as Tenth Street Bootery.

Names of Government Offices

Bureaus, boards, offices, and departments of the city government are filed under the name of the chief governing body. For example: Bureau of the Budget would be filed as if written Budget (Bureau of the).

SAMPLE QUESTION
- A. Jane Earl (2)
- B. James A. Earle (4)
- C. James Earl (1)
- D. J. Earle (3)

The numbers in parentheses show the proper alphabetical order in which these names should be filed. Since the name that should be filed LAST is James A. Earle, the answer to the Sample Question is B.

21.
- A. Corral, Dr. Robert
- B. Carrale, Prof. Robert
- C. Corran, R.
- D. Corret, Ron

22.
- A. Rivera, Ilena
- B. Riviera, Ilene
- C. Rivere, I.
- D. Riviera Ice Cream Co.

23. A. VonHogel, George
    B. Volper, Gary
    C. Vonner, G.
    D. Van Pefel, Gregory

24. A. David Kallish Stationery Co.
    B. Emerson Microfilm Company
    C. David Kalder Industrial Engineers Associated
    D. 5th Avenue Office Furniture Co.

25. A. Bennet, C.
    B. Benett, Chuck
    C. Bennet, Chas.
    D. Bennett, Charles

26. A. The Board of Higher Education
    B. National Education Commission
    C. Eakin, Hugh
    D. Nathan, Ellen

27. A. McCloud, I.
    B. MacGowen, Ian
    C. McGowen, Arthur
    D. Macale, Sean

28. A. Devine, Sarah
    B. Devine, S.
    C. Devine, Sara H.
    D. Devin, Sarah

23.____

24.____

25.____

26.____

27.____

28.____

Questions 29-34.

DIRECTIONS: Questions 29 through 34 are to be answered SOLELY on the basis of the following paragraphs.

A folder is made of a sheet of heavy paper (manila, kraft, pressboard, or red rope stock) that has been folded once so that the back is about one-half inch higher than the front. Folders are larger than the papers they contain in order to protect them. Two standard folder sizes are *letter size* for papers that are 8 1/2" x 11" and *legal size* for papers that are 8 1/2" x 13".

Folders are cut across the top in two ways: so that the back is straight (straight-cut), or so that the back has a tab that projects above the top of the folder. Such tabs bear captions that identify the contents of each folder. Tabs vary in width and position. The tabs of a set of folders that are *one-half cut* are half the width of the folder, and have only two positions.

One-third cut folders have three positions, each tab occupying a third of the width of the folder. Another standard tabbing is *one-fifth cut*, which has five positions. There are also folders with *two-fifths cut*, with the tabs in the third and fourth, or fourth and fifth, positions.

29. Of the following, the BEST title for the above passage is

29.____

A. Filing Folders B. Standard Folder Sizes
C. The Uses of the Folder D. The Use of Tabs

30. According to the above passage, one of the standard folder sizes is called   30.____

    A. kraft cut B. legal cap
    C. one-half cut D. straight-cut

31. According to the above passage, tabs are GENERALLY placed along the _____ of the   31.____
    folder.

    A. back B. front
    C. left side D. right side

32. According to the above passage, a tab is GENERALLY used to   32.____

    A. distinguish between standard folder sizes
    B. identify the contents of a folder
    C. increase the size of the folder
    D. protect the papers within the folder

33. According to the above passage, a folder that is two-fifths cut has _____ tabs.   33.____

    A. no B. two C. three D. five

34. According to the above passage, one reason for making folders larger than the papers   34.____
    they contain is that

    A. only a certain size folder can be made from heavy paper
    B. they will protect the papers
    C. they will aid in setting up a tab system
    D. the back of the folder must be higher than the front

Questions 35-43.

DIRECTIONS: Questions 35 through 43 are to be answered SOLELY on the basis of the following paragraphs.

The City University of New York traces its origins to 1847, when the Free Academy, which later became City College, was founded as the first tuition-free municipal college. City and Hunter Colleges were placed under the direction of the Board of Higher Education in 1926, and Brooklyn and Queens Colleges were subsequently added to the system of municipal colleges. In 1955, Staten Island Community College, the first of the two-year colleges sponsored by the Board of Higher Education under the program of the State University of New York, joined the system.

In 1961, the four senior colleges and three community colleges then under the jurisdiction of the Board of Higher Education became the City University of New York, and a University Graduate Division was organized to offer programs leading to the PhD. Since then, the university has undergone even more rapid growth. Today it consists of nine senior colleges, an upper division college which admits students at the junior level, eight community colleges, a graduate division, and an affiliated medical center.

7 (#2)

In the summer of 1969, the Board of Higher Education resolved that the time had come to commit the resources of the university to meeting an urgent social need unrestricted access to higher education for all youths of the City. Determined to prevent the waste of human potential represented by the thousands of high school graduates whose limited educational opportunities left them unable to meet existing admission standards, the Board moved to adopt a policy of Open Admissions. It was their judgment that the best way of determining whether a potential student can benefit from college work is to admit him to college, provide him with the learning assistance he needs, and then evaluate his performance.

Beginning with the class of June 1970, every New York City resident who received a high school diploma from a public or private high school was guaranteed a place in one of the colleges of City University.

35. Of the following, the BEST title for the above passage is 35.____

    A. A Brief History of the City University
    B. High Schools and the City University
    C. The Components of the University
    D. Tuiton-Free Colleges

36. According to the above passage, which one of the following colleges of the City University was originally called the Free Academy? 36.____
    _____ College

    A. Brooklyn   B. City   C. Hunter   D. Queens

37. According to the above passage, the system of municipal colleges became the City University of New York in 37.____

    A. 1926   B. 1955   C. 1961   D. 1969

38. According to the above passage, Staten Island Community College came under the jurisdiction of the Board of Higher Education 38.____

    A. 6 years after a Graduate Division was organized
    B. 8 years before the adoption of the Open Admissions Policy
    C. 29 years after Brooklyn and Queens Colleges
    D. 29 years after City and Hunter Colleges

39. According to the above passage, the Staten Island Community College is a(n) 39.____

    A. graduate division center
    B. senior college
    C. two-year college
    D. upper division college

40. According to the above passage, the TOTAL number of colleges, divisions, and affiliated branches of the City University is 40.____

    A. 18   B. 19   C. 20   D. 21

41. According to the above passage, the Open Admissions Policy was designed to determine whether a potential student will benefit from college by PRIMARILY 41.____

A. discouraging competition for placement in the City University among high school students
B. evaluating his performance after entry into college
C. lowering admission standards
D. providing learning assistance before entry into college

42. According to the above passage, the FIRST class to be affected by the Open Admissions Policy was the   42._____

    A. high school class which graduated in January 1970
    B. City University class which graduated in June 1970
    C. high school class which graduated in June 1970
    D. City University class which graduated in January 1970

43. According to the above passage, one of the reasons that the Board of Higher Education initiated the policy of Open Admissions was to   43._____

    A. enable high school graduates with a background of limited educational opportunities to enter college
    B. expand the growth of the City University so as to increase the number and variety of degrees offered
    C. provide a social resource to the qualified youth of the City
    D. revise admission standards to meet the needs of the City

Questions 44-50

DIRECTIONS: Questions 44 through 50 are to be answered on the basis of the following table.

DEDUCTIONS

Emp. No.	Name	Exemp	Daily Gross Earnings	Fed. With. Tax	FICA	Grp. Ins.	Hosp.	Bonds	Total Deductions	Net Earnings
123	Anderson, Paul	1	72.50	7.90	3.64	.85	.95		13.34	59.16
209	Greene, Henry	4	85.00	4.00	2.52	.85	.95		8.32	76.68
27	Kowalski, Anna	2	158.33	17.30	8.13	.97	1.10		27.50	130.83
174	Rodriguez, Marie	1	85.00	7.45	2.52	.80	.95		11.72	73.28
362	Rosen, Carl	2	112.28	12.40	5.48	.80	.95		19.63	92.65
198	Sung, Wang Y.	3	95.00	6.00	3.77	.93	1.05	2	13.75	81.25
53	Tomasso, Francis	4	190.81	18.60	8.56	1.12	1.20	3	32.48	158.33
	TOTAL		798.92	73.65	34.62	6.32	7.15	5	126.74	672.18

44. According to the above chart, the sum of the total deductions is APPROXIMATELY _____ percent of the total gross earnings.   44._____

    A. 6.3   B. 9.3   C. 15.8   D. 18.6

45. According to the above chart, the sum of the net earnings of two of the employees is MOST NEARLY the same as the gross earnings of the employee named   45._____

    A. Anna Kowalski   B. Carl Rosen
    C. Marie Rodriguez   D. Wang Y. Sung

46. According to the above chart, the average amount deducted for Federal Withholding Tax of all employees with gross earnings over $100 is 46.____

    A. $5.55   B. $6.33   C. $16.10   D. $17.95

47. According to the above chart, the average net earnings for all employees with net earnings below $100 is APPROXIMATELY 47.____

    A. $67.34   B. $76.60   C. $84.38   D. $96.20

48. According to the above chart, the employee who has the HIGHEST percent of his or her Gross Earnings deducted is 48.____

    A. Paul Anderson   B. Henry Greene
    C. Anna Kowalski   D. Carl Rosen

49. According to the above chart, the number of employees whose Federal Withholding Tax is GREATER than 10% of their gross earnings is 49.____

    A. 2   B. 3   C. 4   D. 5

50. According to the above chart, the Net Earnings of one employee are equal to the Gross Earnings of another employee. 50.____
    The two employees about whom this statement can be made are

    A. Marie Rodriguez and Carl Rosen
    B. Paul Anderson and Henry Greene
    C. Henry Greene and Marie Rodriguez
    D. Anna Kowalski and Francis Tomasso

51. You are preparing a package of six books to mail to a professor who is on sabbatical. They weigh, respectively, 1 pound 11 ounces, 1 pound 6 ounces, 2 pounds 1 ounce, 2 pounds 2 ounces, 1 pound 7 ounces, and 1 pound 8 ounces. The packaging material weighs 6 ounces. 51.____
    The TOTAL weight of the package will be _____ pounds _____ ounces.

    A. 10; 3   B. 10; 9   C. 11; 5   D. 12; 5

52. Part-time students are charged $35.00 per credit for courses at a particular college. In addition, they must pay a $12.00 student activity fee if they take six credits or more and a $7.00 lab fee for each laboratory course. 52.____
    If a person takes one 3-credit course and one 4-credit course and his 4-credit course is a laboratory course, the TOTAL cost to him will be

    A. $252.00   B. $264.00   C. $271.00   D. $276.00

53. The graduating class of a certain community college consisted of 378 majors in secretarial science, 265 majors in engineering science, 57 majors in nursing, 513 majors in accounting, and 865 majors in liberal arts. 53.____
    The percent of students who majored in liberal arts at this college was MOST NEARLY

    A. 24.0%   B. 41.6%   C. 52.3%   D. 71.6%

54. Which one of the following sentences is INCORRECT because of faulty grammar or sentence structure? 54.____

    I. We learned that there was more than ten people present at the conference.

II. Every one of the employees is able to lift the carton.
III. Neither the registrar nor the secretary is in the office today.
IV. The administrative assistant stated that any office assistant who stayed overtime tonight would get a half-day off next month.

The INCORRECT sentence is:

A. I B. II C. III D. IV

55. Which one of the following is the BEST form for the address in a letter? 55._____

   A. Vice President, The Universal Printing Company
      1220 Fifth Avenue
      New York, 10023 New York
   B. Mr. John Jones, Vice President
      The Universal Printing Company
      1220 Fifth Avenue
      New York, New York 10023
   C. Mr. John Jones, Vice President, The Universal
      Printing Company
      1220 Fifth Avenue
      New York, New York 10023
   D. Mr. John Jones Vice President,
      The Universal Printing Company
      1220 Fifth Avenue
      New York, 10023 New York

KEY (CORRECT ANSWERS)

1. A	11. B	21. D	31. A	41. B	51. B
2. A	12. C	22. B	32. B	42. C	52. B
3. B	13. D	23. C	33. B	43. A	53. B
4. C	14. C	24. A	34. B	44. C	54. A
5. D	15. A	25. D	35. A	45. A	55. B
6. A	16. C	26. B	36. B	46. C	
7. B	17. A	27. C	37. C	47. B	
8. A	18. D	28. A	38. D	48. A	
9. B	19. B	29. A	39. C	49. B	
10. B	20. C	30. B	40. C	50. D	

EXAMINATION SECTION
TEST 1

DIRECTIONS: Each question or incomplete statement is followed by several suggested answers or completions. Select the one that BEST answers the question or completes the statement. *PRINT THE LETTER OF THE CORRECT ANSWER IN THE SPACE AT THE RIGHT.*

Questions 1-2.

DIRECTIONS: Questions 1 and 2 are to be answered on the basis of the following conditions.

Assume that you work for Department A, which occupies several floors in one building. There is a reception office on each floor. All visitors (persons not employed in the department) are required to go to the reception office on the same floor as the office of the person they want to see. They sign a register, their presence is announced by the receptionist, and they wait in the reception room for the person they are visiting.

1. As you are walking in the corridor of your department on your way to a meeting in Room 314, a visitor approaches you and asks you to direct her to Room 312. She says that she is delivering some papers to Mr. Crane in that office. The MOST APPROPRIATE action for you to take is to   1.____

    A. offer to deliver the papers to Mr. Crane since you will be passing his office
    B. suggest that she come with you since you will be passing Room 312
    C. direct her to the reception office where Mr. Crane will be contacted for her
    D. take her to the reception office and contact Mr. Crane for her

2. You are acting as receptionist in the reception office on the second floor. A man enters, stating that he is an accountant from another department and that he has an appointment with Mr. Prince, who is located in Room 102 on the first floor.
The BEST action for you to take is to   2.____

    A. phone the reception office on the first floor and ask the receptionist to contact Mr. Prince
    B. advise the man to go to the reception office on the first floor where he will be further assisted
    C. contact Mr. Prince for him and ask that he come to your office where his visitor is waiting
    D. send him directly to Room 102 where he can see Mr. Prince

3. One of the employees whom you supervise complains to you that you give her more work than the other employees and that she cannot finish these assignments by the time you expect them to be completed.
Of the following, the FIRST action you should then take is to   3.____

    A. tell the employee that you expect more work from her because the other employees do not have her capabilities
    B. assure the employee that you always divide the work equally among your subordinates

17

C. review the employee's recent assignments in order to determine whether her complaint is justified
D. ask the employee if there are any personal problems which are interfering with the completion of the assignments

4. Assume that a staff regulation exists which requires an employee to inform his supervisor if the employee will be absent on a particular day.
If an employee fails to follow this regulation, the FIRST action his supervisor should take is to

   A. inform his own supervisor of the situation and ask for further instructions
   B. ask the employee to explain his failure to follow the regulation
   C. tell the employee that another breach of the regulation will lead to disciplinary action
   D. reprimand the employee for failing to follow the regulation

5. An employee tells his supervisor that he submitted an idea to the employees' suggestion program by mail over two months ago and still has not received an indication that the suggestion is being considered. The employee states that when one of his co-workers sent in a suggestion, he received a response within one week. The employee then asks his supervisor what he should do.
Which of the following is the BEST response for the supervisor to make?

   A. "Next time you have a suggestion, see me about it first and I will make sure that it is properly handled."
   B. "I'll try to find out whether your suggestion was received by the program and whether a response was sent."
   C. "Your suggestion probably wasn't that good so there's no sense in pursuing the matter any further."
   D. "Let's get together and submit the suggestion jointly so that it will carry more weight."

6. Assume that you have been trying to teach a newly appointed employee the filing procedures used in your office. The employee seems to be having difficulty learning the procedures even though you consider them relatively simple and you originally learned them in less time than you have already spent trying to teach the new employee.
Before you spend any time trying to teach him any new filing procedures, which of the following actions should you take FIRST?

   A. Try to teach him some other aspect of your office's work.
   B. Tell him that you had little difficulty learning the procedures and ask him why he finds them so hard to learn.
   C. Review with him those procedures you have tried to teach him and determine whether he understands them.
   D. Report to your supervisor that the new employee is unsuited for the work performed in your office.

7. There is a rule in your office that all employees must sign in and out for lunch. You notice that a new employee who is under your direct supervision has not signed in or out for lunch for the past three days. Of the following, the MOST effective action to take is to

A. immediately report this matter to your supervisor
B. note this infraction of rules on the employee's personnel record
C. remind the employee that she must sign in and out for lunch every day
D. send around a memorandum to all employees in the office telling them they must sign in and out for lunch every day

Questions 8-15.

DIRECTIONS: Questions 8 through 15 each show in Column I names written on four cards (lettered w, x, y, z) which have to be filed. You are to choose the option (lettered A, B, C, or D) in Column II which BEST represents the proper order of filing according to the rules and sample question given below. The cards are to be filed according to the following Rules for Alphabetical Filing.

RULES FOR ALPHABETICAL FILING

Names of Individuals

1. The names of individuals are filed in strict alphabetical order, first according to the last name, then according to first name or initial, and finally according to middle name or initial. For example: George Allen precedes Edward Bell and Leonard Reston precedes Lucille Reston.

2. When last names are the same, for example, A. Green and Agnes Green, the one with the initial comes before the one with the name written out when the first initials are identical.

3. When first and last names are the same, a name without a middle initial comes before one with a middle initial. For example: Ralph Simon comes before both Ralph A. Simon and Ralph Adam Simon.

4. When first and last names are the same, a name with a middle initial comes before one with a middle name beginning with the same initial. For example: Sam P. Rogers comes before Sam Paul Rogers.

5. Prefixes such as De , 0', Mac, Mc, and Van are filed as written and are treated as part of the names to which they are connected. For example: Gladys McTeaque is filed before Frances Meadows.

6. Abbreviated names are treated as if they were spelled out. For example: Chas. is filed as Charles and Thos. is filed as Thomas.

7. Titles and designations such as Dr., Mr., and Prof, are ignored in filing.

Names of Organizations

1. The names of business organizations are filed according to the order in which each word in the name appears. When an organization name bears the name of a person, it is filed according to the rules for filing names of people as given above. Vivian Quinn Boutique would, therefore, come before Security Locks Inc. because Quinn comes before Security.

4 (#1)

2. When numerals occur in a name, they are treated as if they were spelled out. For example: 4th Street Thrift Shop is filed as Fourth Street Thrift Shop.

3. When the following words are part of the name of an organization, they are ignored: on, the, of, and.

SAMPLE

	Column I	Column II	The correct way to file the cards is:
w.	Jane Earl	A. w, y, z, x	y. James Earl
x.	James A. Earle	B. y, w, z, x	w. Jane Earl
y.	James Earl	C. x, y, w, z	z. J. Earle
z.	J. Earle	D. x, w, y, z	x. James A. Earle

The correct filing order is shown by the letters, y, w, z, x (in that sequence). Since, in Column II, B appears in front of the letters, y, w, z, x (in that sequence), B is the correct answer to the sample question.

Now answer the following questions using that same procedure.

		Column I		Column II	
8.	w.	James Rothschild	A.	x, z, w, y	8. ___
	x.	Julius B. Rothchild	B.	x, w, z, y	
	y.	B. Rothstein	C.	z, y, w, x	
	z.	Brian Joel Rothenstein	D.	z, w, x, y	
9.	w.	George S. Wise	A.	w, y, z, x	9. ___
	x.	S. G. Wise	B.	x, w, y, z	
	y.	Geo. Stuart Wise	C.	y, x, w, z	
	z.	Prof. Diana Wise	D.	z, w, y, x	
10.	w.	10th Street Bus Terminal	A.	x, z, w, y	10. ___
	x.	Buckingham Travel Agency	B.	y, x, w, z	
	y.	The Buckingham Theater	C.	w, z, y, x	
	z.	Burt Tompkins Studio	D.	x, w, y, z	
11.	w.	National Council of American Importers	A.	w, y, x, z	11. ___
	x.	National Chain Co. of Providence	B.	x, z, w, y	
	y.	National Council on Alcoholism	C.	z, x, w, y	
	z.	National Chain Co.	D.	z, x, y, w	
12.	w.	Dr. Herbert Alvary	A.	w, y, x, z	12. ___
	x.	Mr. Victor Alvarado	B.	z, w, x, y	
	y.	Alvar Industries	C.	y, z, x, w	
	z.	V. Alvarado	D.	w, z, x, y	

	Column I		Column II
13.	w. Joan MacBride x. Wm. Mackey y. Roslyn McKenzie z. Winifred Mackey		A. w, x, z, y B. w, y, z, x C. w, z, x, y D. w, y, x, z	13._____

	Column I		Column II
14.	w. 3 Way Trucking Co. x. 3rd Street Bakery y. 380 Realty Corp. z. Three Lions Pub		A. y, x, z, w B. y, z, w, x C. x, y, z, w D. x, y, w, z	14._____
15.	w. Miss Rose Leonard x. Rev. Leonard Lucas y. Sylvia Leonard Linen Shop z. Rose S. Leonard		A. z, w, x, y B. w, z, y, x C. w, x, z, y D. z, w, y, x	15._____

Questions 16-19.

DIRECTIONS: Answer Questions 16 through 19 ONLY on the basis of the information given in the following passage.

Work measurement concerns accomplishment or productivity. It has to do with results; it does not deal with the amount of energy used up, although in many cases this may be in direct proportion to the work output. Work measurement not only helps a manager to distribute work loads fairly, but it also enables him to define work sueeess in actual units, evaluate employee performance, and determine where corrective help is needed. Work measurement is accomplished by measuring the amount produced, measuring the time spent to produce it, and relating the two. To illustrate, it is common to speak of so many orders processed within a given time. The number of orders processed becomes meaningful when related to the amount of time taken.

Much of the work in an office can be measured fairly accurately and inexpensively. The extent of wo.rk measurement possible in any given case will depend upon the particular type of office tasks performed, but usually from two-thirds to three-fourths of all work in an office can be measured. It is true that difficulty in work measurement is encountered, for example, when the office work is irregular and not repeated often, or when the work is primarily mental rather than manual. These are problems, but they are used as excuses for doing no work measurement far more frequently than is justified.

16. According to the above passage, which of the following BEST illustrates the type of information obtained as a result of work measurement? A   16._____

   A. clerk takes one hour to file 150 folders
   B. typist types five letters
   C. stenographer works harder typing from shorthand notes than she does typing from a typed draft
   D. clerk keeps track of employees' time by computing sick leave, annual leave, and overtime leave

17. The above passage does NOT indicate that work measurement can be used to help a supervisor to determine

    A. why an employee is performing poorly on the job
    B. who are the fast and slow workers in the unit
    C. how the work in the unit should be divided up
    D. how long it should take to perform a certain task

18. According to the above passage, the kind of work that would be MOST difficult to measure would be such work as

    A. sorting mail
    B. designing a form for a new procedure
    C. photocopying various materials
    D. answering inquiries with form letters

19. The excuses mentioned in the above passage for failure to perform work measurement can be BEST summarized as the

    A. repetitive nature of office work
    B. costs involved in carrying out accurate work measurement
    C. inability to properly use the results obtained from work measurement
    D. difficulty involved in measuring certain types of work

Questions 20-24.

DIRECTIONS: In each of Questions 20 through 24, there is a sentence containing one underlined word. Choose the word (lettered A, B, C, or D) which means MOST NEARLY the same as the underlined word as it is used in the sentence.

20. Mr. Warren could not attend the luncheon because he had a prior appointment.

    A. conflicting   B. official
    C. previous   D. important

21. The time allowed to complete the task was not adequate.

    A. long   B. enough   C. excessive   D. required

22. The investigation unit began an extensive search for the information.

    A. complicated   B. superficial
    C. thorough   D. leisurely

23. The secretary answered the telephone in a courteous manner.

    A. businesslike   B. friendly
    C. formal   D. polite

24. The recipient of the money checked the total amount.

    A. receiver   B. carrier   C. borrower   D. giver

25. You receive a telephone call from an employee in another agency requesting information about a project being carried out by a division other than your own. You know little about the work being done, but you would like to help the caller.
Of the following, the BEST action for you to take is to

   A. ask the caller exactly what he would like to know and then tell him all you know about the work being done
   B. ask the caller to tell you exactly what he would like to know so that you can get the information while he waits
   C. tell the caller that you will have the call transferred to the division working on the project
   D. request that the caller write to you so that you can send him the necessary information

25.____

KEY (CORRECT ANSWERS)

1.	C	11.	D
2.	B	12.	C
3.	C	13.	A
4.	B	14.	C
5.	B	15.	B
6.	C	16.	A
7.	C	17.	A
8.	A	18.	B
9.	D	19.	D
10.	B	20.	C

21.	B
22.	C
23.	D
24.	A
25.	C

TEST 2

DIRECTIONS: Each question or incomplete statement is followed by several suggested answers or completions. Select the one that BEST answers the question or completes the statement. *PRINT THE LETTER OF THE CORRECT ANSWER IN THE SPACE AT THE RIGHT.*

1. Which of the following actions by a supervisor is LEAST likely to result in an increase in morale or productivity?   1.___

    A. Delegating additional responsibility but not authority to his subordinates
    B. Spending more time than his subordinates in planning and organizing the office's work
    C. Giving positive rather than negative orders to his subordinates
    D. Keeping his subordinates informed about changes in rules or policies which affect their work

Questions 2-8.

DIRECTIONS: Questions 2 through 8 are based SOLELY on the information and the form given below.

The following form is a Weekly Summary of New Employees and lists all employees appointed to Department F in the week indicated. In addition to the starting date and name, the form includes each new employee's time card number, title, status, work location and supervisor's name.

DEPARTMENT F

Weekly Summary of New Employees — Week Starting March 25

Starting Date	Name Last, First	Time Card No.	Title	Status	Work Location	Supervisor
3/25	Astaire, Hannah	361	Typist	Prov.	Rm. 312	Merrill, Judy
3/25	Silber, Arthur	545	Clerk	Perm.	Rm. 532	Rizzo, Joe
3/26	Vecchio, Robert	620	Accountant	Perm.	Rm. 620	Harper, Ruth
3/26	Goldberg, Sally	373	Stenographer	Prov.	Rm. 308	Merrill, Judy
3/26	Yee, Bruce	555	Accountant	Perm.	Rm. 530	Rizzo, Joe
3/27	Dunning, Betty	469	Typist	Perm.	Rm. 411	Miller, Tony
3/28	Goldman, Sara	576	Stenographer	Prov.	Rm. 532	Rizzo, Joe
3/29	Vesquez, Roy	624	Accountant	Perm.	Rm. 622	Harper, Ruth
3/29	Browning, David	464	Typist	Perm.	Rm. 411	Miller, Tony

2. On which one of the following dates did two employees *in the same title* begin work?   2.____

   A. 3/25   B. 3/26   C. 3/27   D. 3/29

3. To which one of the following supervisors was ONE typist assigned?   3.____

   A. Judy Merrill   B. Tony Miller
   C. Ruth Harper   D. Joe Rizzo

4. Which one of the following supervisors was assigned the GREATEST number of new employees during the week of March 25?   4.____

   A. Ruth Harper   B. Judy Merrill
   C. Tony Miller   D. Joe Rizzo

5. Which one of the following employees was assigned *three days after another employee* to the same job location?   5.____

   A. Sara Goldman   B. David Browning
   C. Bruce Yee   D. Roy Vesquez

6. The title in which BOTH provisional and permanent appointments were made is   6.____

   A. accountant   B. clerk   C. stenographer   D. typist

7. The employee who started work on the SAME day and have the SAME status but DIFFERENT titles are   7.____

   A. Arthur Silber and Hannah Astaire
   B. Robert Vecchio and Bruce Yee
   C. Sally Goldberg and Sara Goldman
   D. Roy Vesquez and David Browning

8. On the basis of the information given on the form, which one of the following conclusions regarding time card numbers appears to be CORRECT?   8.____

   A. The first digit of the time card number is coded according to the assigned title.
   B. The middle digit of the time card number is coded according to the assigned title.
   C. The first digit of the time card number is coded according to the employees' floor locations.
   D. Time card numbers are randomly assigned.

9. Assume that a caller arrives at your desk and states that she is your supervisor's daughter and that she would like to see her father. You have been under the impression that your supervisor has only a two-year-old son.
   Of the following, the BEST way to deal with this visitor is to   9.____

   A. offer her a seat and advise your supervisor of the visitor
   B. tell her to go right in to her father's office
   C. ask her for some proof to show that she is your supervisor's daughter
   D. escort her into your supervisor's office and ask him if the visitor is his daughter

10. Assume that you answer the telephone and the caller says that he is a police officer and asks for personal information about one of your co-workers.   10.____
    Of the following, the BEST course of action for you to take is to

A. give the caller the information he has requested
B. ask the caller for the telephone number of the phone he is using, call him back, and then give him the information
C. refuse to give him any information and offer to transfer the call to your supervisor
D. ask the caller for his name and badge number before giving him the information

Questions 11-16.

DIRECTIONS: Questions 11 through 16 each consist of a sentence which may or may not be an example of good English usage. Consider grammar, punctuation, spelling, capitalization, awkwardness, etc. Examine each sentence, and then choose the correct statement about it from the four choices below it. If the English usage in the sentence given is better than it would be with any of the changes suggested in Options B, C, or D, choose Option A. Do not choose an option that will change the meaning of the sentence.

11. The recruiting officer said, *"There are many different goverment jobs available."* 11.____
    A. This is an example of acceptable writing.
    B. The word *There* should not be capitalized.
    C. The word *goverment* should be spelled *government*.
    D. The comma after the word *said* should be removed.

12. He can recommend a mechanic whose work is reliable. 12.____
    A. This is an example of acceptable writing.
    B. The word *reliable* should be spelled *relyable*.
    C. The word *whose* should be spelled *who's*.
    D. The word *mechanic* should be spelled *mecanic*.

13. She typed quickly; like someone who had not a moment to lose. 13.____
    A. This is an example of acceptable writing.
    B. The word *not* should be removed.
    C. The semicolon should be changed to a comma.
    D. The word *quickly* should be placed before instead of after the word *typed*.

14. She insisted that she had to much work to do. 14.____
    A. This is an example of acceptable writing.
    B. The word *insisted* should be spelled *incisted*.
    C. The word *to* used in front of *much* should be spelled *too*.
    D. The word *do* should be changed to *be done*.

15. He excepted praise from his supervisor for a job well done. 15.____
    A. This is an example of acceptable writing.
    B. The word *excepted* should be spelled *accepted*.
    C. The order of the words *well done* should be changed to *done well*.
    D. There should be a comma after the word *supervisor*

16. What appears to be intentional errors in grammar occur several times in the passage. 16.____

    A. This is an example of acceptable writing.
    B. The word *occur* should be spelled *occurr*.
    C. The word *appears* should be changed to *appear*.
    D. The phrase *several times* should be changed to *from time to time*.

17. The daily compensation to be paid to each consultant hired in a certain agency is computed by dividing his professional earnings in the previous year by 250. The maximum daily compensation they can receive is $200 each. Four consultants who were hired to work on a special project had the following professional earnings in the previous year: $37,500, $44,000, $46,500, and $61,100. 17.____
    What will be the TOTAL DAILY COST to the agency for these four consultants?

    A. $932   B. $824   C. $756   D. $712

18. In a typing and stenographic pool consisting of 30 employees, 2/5 of them are typists, 1/3 of them are senior typists and senior stenographers, and the rest are stenographers. If there are 5 more stenographers than senior stenographers, how many senior stenographers are in the typing and stenographic pool? 18.____

    A. 3   B. 5   C. 8   D. 10

19. There are 3330 copies of a three-page report to be collated. One clerk starts collating at 9:00 A.M. and is joined 15 minutes later by two other clerks. It takes 15 minutes for each of these clerks to collate 90 copies of the report. 19.____
    At what time should the job be completed if ALL three clerks continue working at the SAME rate without breaks?

    A. 12:00 Noon   B. 12:15 P.M.   C. 1:00 P.M.   D. 1:15 P.M.

20. By the end of last year, membership in the blood credit program in a certain agency had increased from the year before by 500, bringing the total to 2500. 20.____
    If the membership increased by the same percentage this year, the TOTAL number of members in the blood credit program for this agency by the end of this year should be

    A. 2625   B. 3000   C. 3125   D. 3250

21. During this year, an agency suggestion program put into practice suggestions from 24 employees, thereby saving the agency 40 times the amount of money it paid in awards. If 1/3 of the employees were awarded $50 each, 1/2 of the employees were awarded $25 each, and the rest were awarded $10 each, how much money did the agency SAVE by using the suggestions? 21.____

    A. $18,760   B. $29,600   C. $32,400   D. $46,740

22. Which of the following actions should a supervisor generally find MOST effective as a method of determining whether subordinates need additional training in performing their work? 22.____

    A. Compiling a list of absences and latenesses of subordinates
    B. Observing the manner in which his subordinates carry out their various tasks
    C. Reviewing the grievances submitted by subordinates
    D. Reminding his subordinates to consult him if they experience difficulty in completing an assignment

23. Of the following types of letters, the MOST difficult to trace if lost after mailing is the _____ letter.

    A. special delivery
    B. registered
    C. insured
    D. certified

24. Suppose that you are looking over a few incoming letters that have been put in your mail basket. You see that one has a return address on the envelope but not on the letter itself. Of the following, the BEST way to make sure there is a correct record of the return address is to

    A. return the letter to the sender and ask him to fill in his address on his own letter
    B. put the letter back into the envelope and close the opening with a paper clip
    C. copy the address onto a 3"x5" index card and throw away the envelope
    D. copy the address onto the letter and staple the envelope to the letter

25. Although most incoming mail that you receive in an office will pertain to business matters, there are times when a letter may be delivered for your supervisor that is marked *Personal*.
    Of the following, the BEST way for you to handle this type of mail is to

    A. open the letter but do not read it, and route it along with the other mail
    B. read the letter to see if it really is personal
    C. have the letter forwarded unopened to your supervisor's home address
    D. deliver the letter to your supervisor's desk unopened

KEY (CORRECT ANSWERS)

1. A	11. C
2. B	12. A
3. A	13. C
4. D	14. C
5. A	15. B
6. D	16. C
7. D	17. D
8. C	18. A
9. A	19. B
10. C	20. C

21. B
22. B
23. D
24. D
25. D

EXAMINATION SECTION
TEST 1

DIRECTIONS: Each question or incomplete statement is followed by several suggested answers or completions. Select the one that BEST answers the question or completes the statement. *PRINT THE LETTER OF THE CORRECT ANSWER IN THE SPACE AT THE RIGHT.*

1. A multi-line telephone with buttons for eight separate lines, plus a *hold* button, is often used when an office requires more than one outside line.
   If you are talking on one line of this type of office phone when another call comes in, what is the procedure to follow if you want to answer the second call but keep the first call on the line?
   Push the
   A. *hold* button at the same time as you push the *pickup* button of the ringing line
   B. *hold* button and then push the *pickup* button of the ringing line
   C. *pickup* button of the ringing line and then push the *hold* button
   D. *pickup* button of the ringing line and push the *hold* button when you return to the original line

   1.____

2. Suppose that you are asked to prepare a petty cash statement for March. The original and one copy are to go to the personnel office. One copy is to go to the fiscal office, and another copy is to go to your supervisor. The last copy is for your files.
   In preparing the statement and the copies, how many sheets of copy paper should you use?
   A. 3   B. 4   C. 5   D. 8

   2.____

3. Which one of the following is the LEAST important advantage of putting the subject of a letter in the heading to the right of the address? It
   A. makes filing of the copy easier
   B. makes more space available in the body of the letter
   C. simplifies distribution of letters
   D. simplifies determination of the subject of the letter

   3.____

4. Of the following, the MOST efficient way to put 100 copies of a one-page letter into 9½" x 4⅛" envelopes for mailing is to fold _____ into an envelope.
   A. each letter and insert it immediately after folding
   B. each letter separately until all 100 are folded; then insert each one
   C. the 100 letters two at a time, then separate them and insert each one
   D. two letters together, slip them apart, and insert each one

   4.____

5. When preparing papers for filing, it is NOT desirable to
   A. smooth papers that are wrinkled
   B. use paper clips to keep related papers together in the files
   C. arrange the papers in the order in which they will be filed
   D. mend torn papers with cellophane tape

6. Of the following, the BEST reason for a clerical unit to have its own duplicating machine is that the unit
   A. uses many forms which it must reproduce internally
   B. must make two copies of each piece of incoming mail for a special file
   C. must make seven copies of each piece of outgoing mail
   D. must type 200 envelopes each month for distribution to the same offices

7. Several offices use the same photocopying machine.
   If each office must pay its share of the cost of running this machine, the BEST way of determining how much of this cost should be charged to each of these offices is to
   A. determine the monthly number of photocopies made by each office
   B. determine the monthly number of originals submitted for photocopying by each office
   C. determine the number of times per day each office uses the photocopying machine
   D. divide the total cost of running the photocopy machine by the total number of offices using the machine

8. Which one of the following would it be BEST to use to indicate that a file folder has been removed from the files for temporary use in another office?
   A(n)
   A. cross-reference card   B. tickler file marker
   C. aperture card   D. out guide

9. Which one of the following is the MOST important objective of filing?
   A. Giving a secretary something to do in her spare time
   B. Making it possible to locate information quickly
   C. Providing a place to store unneeded documents
   D. Keeping extra papers from accumulating on workers' desks

10. If a check has been made out for an incorrect amount, the BEST action for the writer of the check to take is to
    A. erase the original amount and enter the correct amount
    B. cross out the original amount with a single line and enter the correct amount above it
    C. black out the original amount so that it cannot be read and enter the correct amount above it
    D. write a new check

11. Which one of the following BEST describes the usual arrangement of a tickler file?
    A. Alphabetical
    B. Chronological
    C. Numerical
    D. Geographical

11.____

12. Which one of the following is the LEAST desirable filing practice?
    A. Using staples to keep papers together
    B. Filing all material without regard to date
    C. Keeping a record of all materials removed from the files
    D. Writing filing instructions on each paper prior to filing

12.____

13. Assume that one of your duties is to keep records of the office supplies used by your unit for the purpose of ordering new supplies when the old supplies run out.
    The information that will be of MOST help in letting you know when to reorder supplies is the
    A. quantity issued
    B. quantity received
    C. quantity on hand
    D. stock number

13.____

Questions 14-19.

DIRECTIONS: Questions 14 through 19 consist of sets of names and addresses. In each question, the name and address in Column II should be an exact copy of the name and address in Column I. If there is
a mistake *only* in the name, mark your answer A;
a mistake *only* in the address, mark your answer B;
a mistake in *both* name and address, mark your answer C;
no mistake in either name or address, mark your answer D.

SAMPLE QUESTION

Column I
Michael Filbert
456 Reade Street
New York, N.Y. 10013

Column II
Michael Filbert
645 Reade Street
New York, N.Y. 10013

Since there is a mistake only in the address (the street number should be 456 instead of 645), the answer to the sample question is B.

COLUMN I

COLUMN II

14. Esta Wong
    141 West 68 St.
    New York, N.Y. 10023

    Esta Wang
    141 West 68 St.
    New York,, N.Y. 10023

14.____

15. Dr. Alberto Grosso
    3475 12th Avenue
    Brooklyn, N.Y. 11218

    Dr. Alberto Grosso
    3475 12th Avenue
    Brooklyn, N.Y. 11218

15.____

	Column I	Column II	
16.	Mrs. Ruth Bortlas 482 Theresa Ct. Far Rockaway, N.Y. 11691	Ms. Ruth Bortlas 482 Theresa Ct. Far Rockaway, N.Y. 11169	16._____
17.	Mr. and Mrs. Howard Fox 2301 Sedgwick Avenue Bronx, N.Y. 10468	Mr. and Mrs. Howard Fox 231 Sedgwick Ave. Bronx, N.Y. 10458	17._____
18.	Miss Marjorie Black 223 East 23 Street New York, N.Y. 10010	Miss Margorie Black 223 East 23 Street New York, N.Y. 10010	18._____
19.	Michelle Herman 806 Valley Rd. Old Tappan, N.J. 07675	Michelle Hermann 806 Valley Dr. Old Tappan, N.J. 07675	19._____

Questions 20-25.

DIRECTIONS: Questions 20 through 25 are to be answered SOLELY on the basis of the information in the following passage.

Basic to every office is the need for proper lighting. Inadequate lighting is a familiar cause of fatigue and serves to create a somewhat dismal atmosphere in the office. One requirement of proper lighting is that it be of an appropriate intensity. Intensity is measured in foot-candles. According to the Illuminating Engineering Society of New York, for casual seeing tasks such as in reception rooms, inactive file rooms, and other service areas, it is recommended that the amount of light be 30 foot-candles. For ordinary seeing tasks such as reading and work in active file rooms and in mail rooms, the recommended lighting is 100 foot-candles. For very difficult seeing tasks such as accounting, transcribing, and business machine use, the recommended lighting is 150 foot-candles.

Lighting intensity is only one requirement. Shadows and glare are to be avoided. For example, the larger the proportion of a ceiling filled with lighting units, the more glare-free and comfortable the lighting will be. Natural lighting from windows is not too dependable because on dark wintry days, windows yield little usable light, and on sunny afternoons, the glare from windows may be very distracting. Desks should not face the windows. Finally, the main lighting source ought to be overhead and to the left of the user.

20. According to the above passage, insufficient light in the office may cause 20._____
   A. glare
   B. shadows
   C. tiredness
   D. distraction

21. Based on the above passage, which of the following must be considered when planning lighting arrangements? 21._____
   The
   A. amount of natural light present
   B. amount of work to be done
   C. level of difficulty of work to be done
   D. type of activity to be carried out

22. It can be inferred from the above passage that a well-coordinated lighting scheme is LIKELY to result in
    A. greater employee productivity
    B. elimination of light reflection
    C. lower lighting cost
    D. more use of natural light

23. Of the following, the BEST title for the above passage is
    A. Characteristics of Light
    B. Light Measurement Devices
    C. Factors to Consider When Planning Lighting Systems
    D. Comfort vs. Cost When Devising Lighting Arrangements

24. According to the above passage, a foot-candle is a measurement of the
    A. number of bulbs used
    B. strength of the light
    C. contrast between glare and shadow
    D. proportion of the ceiling filled with lighting units

25. According to the above passage, the number of foot-candles of light that would be needed to copy figures onto a payroll is _____ foot-candles.
    A. less than 30   B. 30   C. 100   D. 150

KEY (CORRECT ANSWERS)

1.	B		11.	B
2.	B		12.	B
3.	B		13.	C
4.	A		14.	A
5.	B		15.	D
6.	A		16.	C
7.	A		17.	B
8.	D		18.	A
9.	B		19.	C
10.	D		20.	C

21.	D
22.	A
23.	C
24.	B
25.	D

TEST 2

DIRECTIONS: Each question or incomplete statement is followed by several suggested answers or completions. Select the one that BEST answers the question or completes the statement. *PRINT THE LETTER OF THE CORRECT ANSWER IN THE SPACE AT THE RIGHT.*

1. Assume that a supervisor has three subordinates who perform clerical tasks. One of the employees retires and is replaced by someone who is transferred from another unit in the agency. The transferred employee tells the supervisor that she has worked as a clerical employee for two years and understands clerical operations quite well. The supervisor then assigns the transferred employee to a desk, tells the employee to begin working, and returns to his own desk.
The supervisor's action in this situation is
    A. *proper;* experienced clerical employees do not require training when they are transferred to new assignments
    B. *improper;* before the supervisor returns to his desk, he should tell the other two subordinates to watch the transferred employee perform the work
    C. *proper;* if the transferred employee makes any mistakes, she will bring them to the supervisor's attention
    D. *improper;* the supervisor should find out what clerical tasks the transferred employee has performed and give her instruction in those which are new or different

1.____

2. Assume that you are falling behind in completing your work assignments and you believe that your workload is too heavy.
Of the following, the BEST course of action for you to take FIRST is to
    A. discuss the problem with your supervisor
    B. decide which of your assignments can be postponed
    C. try to get some of your co-workers to help you out
    D. plan to take some of the work home with you in order to catch up

2.____

3. Suppose that one of the clerks under your supervision is filling in monthly personnel forms. She asks you to explain a particular personnel regulation which is related to various items on the forms. You are not thoroughly familiar with the regulation.
Of the following responses you may make, the one which will gain the MOST respect from the clerk and which is generally the MOST advisable is to
    A. tell the clerk to do the best she can and that you will check her work later
    B. inform the clerk that you are not sure of a correct explanation but suggest a procedure for her to follow
    C. give the clerk a suitable interpretation so that she will think you are familiar with all regulations
    D. tell the clerk that you will have to read the regulation more thoroughly before you can give her an explanation

3.____

4. Charging out records until a specified due date, with prompt follow-up if they are not returned, is a 4.____
   A. *good* idea; it may prevent the records from being kept needlessly on someone's desk for long periods of time
   B. *good* idea; it will indicate the extent of your authority to other departments
   C. *poor* idea; the person borrowing the material may make an error because of the pressure put upon him to return the records
   D. *poor* idea; other departments will feel that you do not trust them with the records and they will be resentful

Questions 5-9.

DIRECTIONS: Questions 5 through 9 consist of three lines of code letters and numbers. The numbers on each line should correspond with the code letters on the same line in accordance with the table below.

Code Letter	P	L	I	J	B	O	H	U	C	G
Corresponding Letter	0	1	2	3	4	5	6	7	8	9

On some of the lines, an error exists in the coding. Compare the letters and numbers in each question carefully. If you find an error or errors on
   only one of the lines in the question, mark your answer A;
   any two lines in the question, mark your answer B;
   all three lines in the question, mark your answer C;
   none of the lines in the question, mark your answer D.

SAMPLE QUESTION
JHOILCP   3652180
BICLGUP   4286970
UCIBHLJ   5824613

In the above sample, the first line is correct since each code letter listed has the correct corresponding number. On the second line, an error exists because code letter L should have the number 1 instead of the number 6. On the third line, an error exists because the code letter U should have the number 7 instead of the number 5. Since there are errors on two of the three lines, the correct answer is B.

5. BULJCIP   4713920   5.____
    HIGPOUL   6290571
    OCUHJJBI   5876342

6. CUBLOIJ   8741023   6.____
    LCLGCLB   1818914
    JPUHIOC   3076158

7. OIJGCBPO   52398405   7.____
    UHPBLIOP   76041250
    CLUIPGPC   81720908

35

8. BPCOUOJI   40875732
    UOHCIPLB   75682014
    GLHUUCBJ   92677843

9. HOIOHJLH   65256361
    IOJJHHBP   25536640
    OJHBJOPI   53642502

Questions 10-13.

DIRECTIONS: Questions 10 through 13 are to be answered SOLELY on the basis of the information given in the following passage.

The mental attitude of the employee toward safety is exceedingly important in preventing accidents. All efforts designed to keep safety on the employee's mind and to keep accident prevention a live subject in the office will help substantially in a safety program. Although it may seem strange, it is common for people to be careless. Therefore, safety education is a continuous process.

Safety rules should be explained, and the reasons for their rigid enforcement should be given to employees. Telling employees to be careful or giving similar general safety warnings and slogans is probably of little value. Employees should be informed of basic safety fundamentals. This can be done through staff meetings, informal suggestions to employees, movies, and safety instruction cards. Safety instruction cards provide the employees with specific suggestions about safety and serve as a series of timely reminder helping to keep safety on the minds of employees. Pictures, posters, and cartoon sketches on bulletin boards that are located in areas continually used by employees arouse the employees' interest in safety. It is usually good to supplement this type of safety promotion with intensive individual follow-up.

10. The above passage implies that the LEAST effective of the following safety measures is
    A. rigid enforcement of safety rules
    B. getting employees to think in terms of safety
    C. elimination of unsafe conditions in the office
    D. telling employees to stay alert at all times

11. The reason given by the passage for maintaining ongoing safety education is that
    A. people are often careless
    B. office tasks are often dangerous
    C. the value of safety slogans increases with repetition
    D. safety rules change frequently

12. Which one of the following safety aids is MOST likely to be preferred by the passage? A
    A. cartoon of a man tripping over a carton and yelling, *Keep aisles clear!*
    B. poster with a large number one and a caption saying, *Safety First*

C. photograph of a very neatly arranged office
D. large sign with the word *THINK* in capital letters

13. Of the following, the BEST title for the above passage is 13.____
    A. Basic Safety Fundamentals
    B. Enforcing Safety Among Careless Employees
    C. Attitudes Toward Safety
    D. Making Employees Aware of Safety

Questions 14-21.

DIRECTIONS: Questions 14 through 21 are to be answered SOLELY on the basis of the information and chart given below.

The following chart shows expenses in five selected categories for a one-year period, expressed as percentages of these same expenses during the previous year. The chart compares two different offices. In Office T (represented by ▓▓▓▓), a cost reduction program has been tested for the past year. The other office, Office Q (represented by ▨▨▨▨), served as a control, in that no special effort was made to reduce costs during the past year.

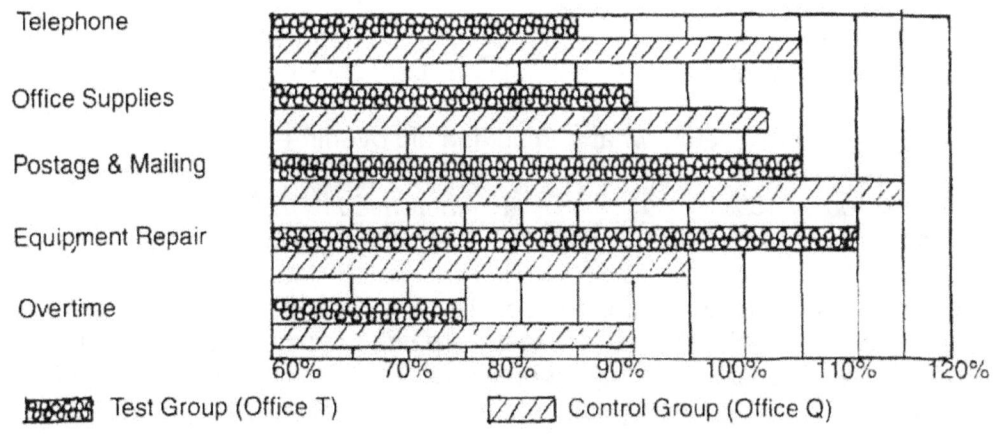

RESULTS OF OFFICE COST REDUCTION PROGRAM
Expenses of Test and Control Groups for 2020
Expressed as Percentages of Same Expenses for 2019

14. In Office T, which category of expense showed the greatest percentage REDUCTION from 2019 to 2020? 14.____
    A. Telephone   B. Office Supplies
    C. Postage & Mailing   D. Overtime

15. In which expense category did Office T show the BEST results in percentage terms when compared to Office Q? 15.____
    A. Telephone   B. Office Supplies
    C. Postage & Mailing   D. Overtime

5 (#2)

16. According to the above chart, the cost reduction program was LEAST effective for the expense category of
    A. Office Supplies
    B. Postage & Mailing
    C. Equipment Repair
    D. Overtime

17. Office T's telephone costs went down during 2020 by approximately how many percentage points?
    A. 15
    B. 20
    C. 85
    D. 104

18. Which of the following changes occurred in expenses for Office Supplies in Office Q in the year 2020 as compared with the year 2019?
    They
    A. increased by more than 100%
    B. remained the same
    C. decreased by a few percentage points
    D. increased by a few percentage points

19. For which of the following expense categories do the results in Office T and the results in Office Q differ MOST NEARLYY by 10 percentage points?
    A. Telephone
    B. Postage & Mailing
    C. Equipment Repair
    D. Overtime

20. In which expense category did Office Q's costs show the GREATEST percentage increase in 2020?
    A. Telephone
    B. Office Supplies
    C. Postage & Mailing
    D. Equipment Repair

21. In Office T, by approximately what percentage did overtime expense change during the past year? It
    A. *increased* by 15%
    B. *increased* by 75%
    C. *decreased* by 10%
    D. *decreased* by 25%

22. In a particular agency, there were 160 accidents in 2017. Of these accidents, 75% were due to unsafe acts and the rest were due to unsafe conditions. In the following year, a special safety program was established. The number of accidents in 2019 due to unsafe acts was reduced to 35% of what it had been in 2017.
    How many accidents due to unsafe acts were there in 2019?
    A. 20
    B. 36
    C. 42
    D. 56

23. At the end of every month, the petty cash fund of Agency A is reimbursed for payments made from the fund during the month. During the month of February, the amounts paid from the fund were entered on receipts as follows: 10 bus fares of $3.50 each and one taxi fare of $35.00. At the end of the month, the money left in the fund was in the following denominations: 15 ten-dollar bills, 10 one-dollar bills, 40 quarters, and 100 dimes.
    If the petty cash fund is reduced by 20% for the following month, how much money will there be available in the petty cash fund for March?
    A. $110.00
    B. $200.00
    C. $215.00
    D. $250.00

24. The one of the following records which it would be MOST advisable to keep in alphabetical order is a
    A. continuous listing of phone messages, including time and caller, for your supervisor
    B. listing of individuals currently employed by your agency in a particular title
    C. record of purchases paid for by the petty cash fund
    D. dated record of employees who have borrowed material from the files in your office

25. Assume that you have been asked to copy by hand a column of numbers with two decimal places from one record to another. Each number consists of three, four, and five digits.
    In order to copy them quickly and accurately, you should copy
    A. each number exactly, making sure that the column of digits farthest to the right is in a straight line and all other columns are lined up
    B. the column of digits farthest to the right and then copy the next column of digits moving from right to left
    C. the column of digits farthest to the left and then copy the next column of digits moving from left to right
    D. the digits to the right of each decimal point and then copy the digits to the left of each decimal point

KEY (CORRECT ANSWERS)

1.	D		11.	A
2.	A		12.	A
3.	D		13.	D
4.	A		14.	D
5.	A		15.	A
6.	C		16.	C
7.	D		17.	A
8.	B		18.	D
9.	C		19.	B
10.	D		20.	C

21.	D
22.	C
23.	B
24.	B
25.	A

EXAMINATION SECTION

TEST 1

DIRECTIONS: Each question or incomplete statement is followed by several suggested answers or completions. Select the one that BEST answers the question or completes the statement. *PRINT THE LETTER OF THE CORRECT ANSWER IN THE SPACE AT THE RIGHT.*

1. Assume that a few co-workers meet near your desk and talk about personal matters during working hours. Lately, this practice has interfered with your work. In order to stop this practice, the BEST action for you to take FIRST is to
    A. ask your supervisor to put a stop to the co-workers' meeting near your desk
    B. discontinue any friendship with this group
    C. ask your co-workers not to meet near your desk
    D. request that your desk be moved to another location

1._____

2. In order to maintain office coverage during working hours, your supervisor has scheduled your lunch hour from 1 P.M. to 2 P.M. and your co-workers' lunch hour from 12 P.M. to 1 P.M. Lately, your co-worker has been returning late from lunch each day. As a result, you don't get a full hour since you must return to the office by 2 P.M.
    Of the following, the BEST action for you to take FIRST is to
    A. explain to your co-worker in a courteous manner that his lateness is interfering with your right to a full hour for lunch
    B. tell your co-worker that his lateness must stop or you will report him to your supervisor
    C. report your co-worker's lateness to your supervisor
    D. leave at 1 P.M. for lunch, whether your co-worker has returned or not

2._____

3. Assume that, as an office worker, one of your jobs is to open mail sent to your unit, read the mail for content, and send the mail to the appropriate person to handle. You accidentally open and begin to read a letter marked *personal* to a co-worker.
    Of the following, the BEST action for you to take is to
    A. report to your supervisor that your co-worker is receiving personal mail at the office
    B. destroy the letter so that your co-worker does not know you saw it
    C. reseal the letter and place it on the co-worker's desk without saying anything
    D. bring the letter to your co-worker and explain that you opened it by accident

3._____

4. Suppose that in evaluating your work, your supervisor gives you an overall rating, but states that you sometimes turn in work with careless errors.
The BEST action for you to take would be to
   A. ask a co-worker who is good at details to proofread your work
   B. take time to do a careful job, paying more attention to detail
   C. continue working as usual since occasional errors are to be expected
   D. ask your supervisor if she would mind correcting your errors

5. Assume that you are taking a telephone message for a co-worker who is not in the office at the time.
Of the following, the LEAST important item to write on the message is the
   A. length of the call   B. name of the caller
   C. time of the call   D. telephone number of the caller

Questions 6-13.

DIRECTIONS: Questions 6 through 13 each consist of a sentence which may or may not be an example of good English. The underlined parts of each sentence may be correct or incorrect. Examine each sentence, considering grammar, punctuation, spelling, and capitalization. If the English usage in the underlined parts of the sentence given is better than any of the changes in the underlined words suggested in Options B, C, or D, choose Option A. If the changes in the underlined words suggested in Options B, C, or D would make the sentence correct, choose the correct option. Do not choose an option that will change the meaning of the sentence.

6. This Fall, the office will be closed on Columbus Day, October 9th.
   A. Correct as is   B. fall...Columbus Day, October
   C. Fall...Columbus day, October   D. fall...Columbus Day, october

7. This manual discribes the duties performed by an Office Aide.
   A. Correct as is   B. describe the duties performed
   C. discribe the duties performed   D. describes the duties performed

8. There weren't no paper in the supply closet.
   A. Correct as is   B. weren't any
   C. wasn't any   D. wasn't no

9. The new employees left there office to attend a meeting.
   A. Correct as is   B. they're
   C. their   D. thier

10. The office worker started working at 8:30 a.m.
    A. Correct as is   B. 8:30 a.m.
    C. 8;30 a,m.   D. 8:30 am.

11. The alphabet, or A to Z sequence are the basis of most filing systems.
    A. Correct as is   B. alphabet, or A to Z sequence, is
    C. alphabet, or A to Z sequence are   D. alphabet, or A too Z sequence, is

12. Those file cabinets are five feet tall. 12.____
    A. Correct as is   B. Them…feet
    C. Those…foot   D. Them…foot

13. The Office Aide checked the register and finding the date of the meeting. 13.____
    A. Correct as is   B. regaster and finding
    C. register and found   D. regaster and found

Questions 14-21.

DIRECTIONS: Each of Questions 14 through 21 has two lists of numbers. Each list contains three sets of numbers. Check each of the three sets in the list on the right to see if they are the same as the corresponding set in the list on the left. Mark your answers
    A. if none of the sets in the right list are the same as those in the left list
    B. if only one of the sets in the right list are the same as those in the left list
    C. if only two of the sets in the right list are the same as those in the left list
    D. if all three sets in the right list are the same as those in the left list

14. 7354183476   7354983476   14.____
      4474747744   4474747774
      57914302311   57914302311

15. 7143592185   7143892185   15.____
      8344517699   8344518699
      9178531263   9178531263

16. 2572114731   257214731   16.____
      8806835476   8806835476
      8255831246   8255831246

17. 331476853821   331476858621   17.____
      6976658532996   6976655832996
      3766042113715   3766042113745

18. 8806663315   8806663315   18.____
      74477138449   74477138449
      211756663666   211756663666

19. 990006966996   99000696996   19.____
      53022219743   53022219843
      4171171117717   4171171177717

20. 24400222433004   24400222433004   20.____
      5300030055000355 5300030055500355
      20000075532002022 20000075532002022

21. 6111666406600011116   61116664066001116   21.____
     7111300117001100733   7111300117001100733
     26666446664476518   26666446664476518

Questions 22-25.

DIRECTIONS: Each of Questions 22 through 25 has two lists of names and addresses. Each
list contains three sets of names and addresses. Check each of the three sets
in the list on the right to see if they are the same as the corresponding set in
the list on the left. Mark your answers
    A. if none of the sets in the right list are the same as those in the left list
    B. if only one of the sets in the right list are the same as those in the left list
    C. if only two of the sets in the right list are the same as those in the left list
    D. if all three sets in the right list are the same as those in the left list

22. Mary T. Berlinger   Mary T. Berlinger   22.____
     2351 Hampton St.   2351 Hampton St.
     Monsey, N.Y. 20117   Monsey, N.Y. 20117

     Eduardo Benes   Eduardo Benes
     473 Kingston Avenue   473 Kingston Avenue
     Central Islip, N.Y. 11734   Central Islip, N.Y. 11734

     Alan Carrington Fuchs   Alan Carrington Fuchs
     17 Gnarled Hollow Road   17 Gnarled Hollow Road
     Los Angeles, CA 91635   Los Angeles, CA 91685

23. David John Jacobson   David John Jacobson   23.____
     178 35 St. Apt. 4C   178 53 St. Apt. 4C
     New York, N.Y. 00927   New York, N.Y. 00927

     Ann-Marie Calonella   Ann-Marie Calonella
     7243 South Ridge Blvd.   7243 South Ridge Blvd.
     Bakersfield, CA 96714   Bakersfield, CA 96714

     Pauline M. Thompson   Pauline M. Thomson
     872 Linden Ave.   872 Linden Ave.
     Houston, Texas 70321   Houston, Texas 70321

24. Chester LeRoy Masterton   Chester LeRoy Masterson   24.____
     152 Lacy Rd.   152 Lacy Rd.
     Kankakee, Ill. 54532   Kankakee, Ill. 54532

     William Maloney   William Maloney
     S. LaCrosse Pla.   S. LaCross Pla.
     Wausau, Wisconsin 52146   Wausau, Wisconsin 52146

5 (#1)

	Cynthia V. Barnes 16 Pines Rd. Greenpoint, Miss. 20376	Cynthia V. Barnes 16 Pines Rd. Greenpoint, Miss. 20376	
25.	Marcel Jean Frontenac 6 Burton On The Water Calender, Me. 01471	Marcel Jean Frontenac 6 Burton On The Water Calender, Me. 01471	25.____
	J. Scott Marsden 174 S. Tipton St. Cleveland, Ohio	J. Scott Marsden 174 Tipton St. Cleveland, Ohio	
	Lawrence T. Haney 171 McDonough St. Decatur, Ga. 31304	Lawrence T. Haney 171 McDonough St. Decatur, Ga. 31304	

KEY (CORRECT ANSWERS)

1.	C		11.	B
2.	A		12.	A
3.	D		13.	C
4.	B		14.	B
5.	A		15.	B
6.	B		16.	C
7.	D		17.	A
8.	C		18.	D
9.	C		19.	A
10.	B		20.	C

21. C
22. C
23. B
24. B
25. C

TEST 2

DIRECTIONS: Each question or incomplete statement is followed by several suggested answers or completions. Select the one that BEST answers the question or completes the statement. *PRINT THE LETTER OF THE CORRECT ANSWER IN THE SPACE AT THE RIGHT.*

Questions 1-6.

DIRECTIONS: Questions 1 through 6 are to be answered SOLELY on the basis of the information contained in the following passage.

Duplicating is the process of making a number of identical copies of letters, document, etc. from an original. Some duplicating processes make copies directly from the original document. Other duplicating processes require the preparation of a special master, and copies are then made from the master. Four of the most common duplicating processes are stencil, fluid, offset, and xerox.

In the stencil process, the typewriter is used to cut the words into a master called a stencil. Drawings, charts, or graphs can be cut into the stencil using a stylus. As many as 3,500 good-quality copies can be reproduced from one stencil. Various grades of finished paper from inexpensive mimeograph to expensive bond can be used.

The fluid process is a good method of copying from 50 to 125 good-quality copies from a master, which is prepared with a special dye. The master is placed on the duplicator, and special paper with a hard finish is moistened and then passed through the duplicator. Some of the dye on the master is dissolved, creating an impression on the paper. The impression becomes lighter as more copies are made; and once the dye on the master is used up, a new master must be made.

The offset process is the most adaptable office duplicating process because this process can be used for making a few copies or many copies. Masters can be made on paper or plastic for a few hundred copies, or on metal plates for as many as 75,000 copies. By using a special technique called photo-offset, charts, photographs, illustrations, or graphs can be reproduced on the master plate. The offset process is capable of producing large quantities of fine, top-quality copies on all types of finished paper.

The xerox process reproduces an exact duplicate from an original. It is the fastest duplicating method because the original material is placed directly on the duplicator, eliminating the need to make a special master. Any kind of paper can be used. The xerox process is the most expensive duplicating process; however, it is the best method of reproducing small quantities of good-quality copies of reports, letters, official documents, memos, or contracts.

1. Of the following, the MOST efficient method of reproducing 5,000 copies of a graph is
   A. stencil   B. fluid   C. offset   D. xerox

1._____

2. The offset process is the MOST adaptable office duplicating process because
   A. it is the quickest duplicating method
   B. it is the least expensive duplicating method
   C. it can produce a small number or large number of copies
   D. a softer master can be used over and over again

3. Which one of the following duplicating processes uses moistened paper?
   A. Stencil   B. Fluid   C. Offset   D. Xerox

4. The fluid process would be the BEST process to use for reproducing
   A. five copies of a school transcript
   B. fifty copies of a memo
   C. five hundred copies of a form letter
   D. five thousand copies of a chart

5. Which one of the following duplicating processes does NOT require a special master?
   A. Fluid   B. Xerox   C. Offset   D. Stencil

6. Xerox is NOT used for all duplicating jobs because
   A. it produces poor-quality copies
   B. the process is too expensive
   C. preparing the master is too time-consuming
   D. it cannot produce written reports

7. Assume a city agency has 775 office workers.
   If 2 out of 25 office workers were absent on a particular day, how many office workers reported to work on that day?
   A. 713   B. 744   C. 750   D. 773

Questions 8-11.

DIRECTIONS: In Questions 8 through 11, select the choice that is CLOSEST in meaning to the underlined word.

   SAMPLE: This division reviews the fiscal reports of the agency.
   In this sentence, the word *fiscal* means MOST NEARLY
   A. financial   B. critical   C. basic   D. personnel

   The correct answer is A, financial, because financial is closest to *fiscal*.

8. A central file eliminates the need to retain duplicate material.
   The word *retain* means MOST NEARLY
   A. keep   B. change   C. locate   D. process

9. Filing is a routine office task.
   Routine means MOST NEARLY
   A. proper   B. regular   C. simple   D. difficult

10. Sometimes a word, phrase, or sentence must be <u>deleted</u> to correct an error. 10.____
    Deleted means MOST NEARLY
    A. removed   B. added   C. expanded   D. improved

11. Your supervisor will <u>evaluate</u> your work. 11.____
    Evaluate means MOST NEARLY
    A. judge   B. list   C. assign   D. explain

Questions 12-19.

DIRECTIONS: The code table below shows 10 letters with matching numbers. For each Question 12 through 19, there are three sets of letters. Each set of letters is followed by a set of numbers which may or may not match their correct letter according to the code table. For each question, check all three sets of letters and numbers and mark your answer
    A. if no pairs are correctly matched
    B. if only one pair is correctly matched
    C. if only two pairs are correctly matched
    D. if all three pairs are correctly matched

CODE TABLE

T	M	V	D	S	P	R	G	B	H
1	2	3	4	5	6	7	8	9	0

SAMPLE QUESTION: TMVDSP   123456
                    RGBHTM   789011
                    DSPRGB   256789

In the sample question above, the first set of numbers correctly matches its set of letters. But the second and third pairs contain mistakes. In the second pair, M is incorrectly matched with number 1. According to the code table, letter M should be correctly matched with number 2. In the third pair, the letter D is incorrectly matched with number 2. According to the code table, letter D should be correctly matched with number 4. Since only one of the pairs is correctly matched, the answer to this sample question is B.

12. RSBMRM   759262   12.____
    GDSRVH   845730
    VDBRTM   349713

13. TGVSDR   183247   13.____
    SMHRDP   520647
    TRMHSR   172057

14. DSPRGM   456782   14.____
    MVDBHT   234902
    HPMDBT   062491

15.	BVPTRD	936184	15._____
	GDPHMB	807029	
	GMRHMV	827032	
16.	MGVRSH	283750	16._____
	TRDMBS	174295	
	SPRMGV	567283	
17.	SGBSDM	489542	17._____
	MGHPTM	290612	
	MPBMHT	269301	
18.	TDPBHM	146902	18._____
	VPBMRS	369275	
	GDMBHM	842902	
19.	MVPTBV	236194	19._____
	PDRTMB	647128	
	BGTMSM	981232	

Questions 20-25.

DIRECTIONS: In each of Questions 20 through 25, the names of four people are given. For each question, choose as your answer the one of the four names given which should be filed FIRST according to the usual system of alphabetical filing of names, as described in the following paragraph.

In filing names, you must start with the last name. Names are filed in order of the first letter of the last name, then the second letter, etc. Therefore, BAILY would be filed before BROWN, which would be filed before COLT. A name with fewer letters of the same type comes first; i.e., Smith before Smithe. If the last names are the same, the names are filed alphabetically by the first name. If the first name is an initial, a name with an initial would come before a first name that starts with the same letter as the initial. Therefore, I. BROWN would come before IRA BROWN. Finally, if both last name and first name are the same, the name would be filed alphabetically by the middle name, one again an initial coming before a middle name which starts with the same letter as the initial. If there is no middle name at all, the name would come before those with middle initials or names.

SAMPLE QUESTION: A. Lester Daniels
B. William Dancer
C. Nathan Danzig
D. Dan Lester

The last names beginning with D are filed before the last name beginning with L. Since DANIELS, DANCER, and DANZIG all begin with the same three letters, you must look at the fourth letter of the last name to determine which name should be filed first. C comes before I or Z in the alphabet, so DANCER is filed before DANIELS or DANZIG. Therefore, the answer to the above sample question is B.

20. A. Scott Biala   B. Mary Byala   20._____
    C. Martin Baylor   D. Francis Bauer

21. A. Howard J. Black   B. Howard Black   21._____
    C. J. Howard Black   D. John H. Black

22. A. Theodora Garth Kingston   B. Theadore Barth Kingston   22._____
    C. Thomas Kingston   D. Thomas T. Kingston

23. A. Paulette Mary Huerta   B. Paul M. Huerta   23._____
    C. Paulette L. Huerta   D. Peter A. Huerta

24. A. Martha Hunt Morgan   B. Martin Hunt Morgan   24._____
    C. Mary H. Morgan   D. Martine H. Morgan

25. A. James T. Meerschaum   B. James M. Mershum   25._____
    C. James F. Mearshaum   D. James N. Meshum

KEY (CORRECT ANSWERS)

1.	C		11.	A
2.	C		12.	B
3.	B		13.	B
4.	B		14.	C
5.	B		15.	A
6.	B		16.	D
7.	A		17.	A
8.	A		18.	D
9.	B		19.	A
10.	A		20.	D

21. B
22. B
23. B
24. A
25. C

TEST 3

DIRECTIONS: Each question or incomplete statement is followed by several suggested answers or completions. Select the one that BEST answers the question or completes the statement. *PRINT THE LETTER OF THE CORRECT ANSWER IN THE SPACE AT THE RIGHT.*

1. Which one of the following statements about proper telephone usage is NOT always correct?
   When answering the telephone, you should
   A. know whom you are speaking to
   B. give the caller your undivided attention
   C. identify yourself to the caller
   D. obtain the information the caller wishes before you do your other work

   1._____

2. Assume that, as a member of a worker's safety committee in your agency, you are responsible for encouraging other employees to follow correct safety practices. While you are working on your regular assignment, you observe an employee violating a safety rule.
   Of the following, the BEST action for you to take FIRST is to
   A. speak to the employee about safety practices and order him to stop violating the safety rule
   B. speak to the employee about safety practices and point out the safety rule he is violating
   C. bring the matter up in the next committee meeting
   D. report this violation of the safety rule to the employee's supervisor

   2._____

3. Assume that you have been temporarily assigned by your supervisor to do a job which you do not want to do.
   The BEST action for you to take is to
   A. discuss the job with your supervisor, explaining why you do not want to do it
   B. discuss the job with your supervisor and tell her that you will not do it
   C. ask a co-worker to take your place on this job
   D. do some other job that you like; your supervisor may give the job you do not like to someone else

   3._____

4. Assume that you keep the confidential personnel files of employees in your unit. A friend asks you to obtain some information from the file of one of your co-workers.
   The BEST action to take is to _____ to your friend.
   A. ask the co-worker if you can give the information
   B. ask your supervisor if you can give the information
   C. give the information
   D. refuse to give the information

   4._____

Questions 5-8.

DIRECTIONS: Questions 5 through 8 are to be answered SOLELY on the basis of the information contained in the following passage.

City government is committed to providing a safe and healthy work environment for all city employees. An effective agency safety program reduces accidents by educating employees about the types of careless acts which can cause accidents. Even in an office, accidents can happen. If each employee is aware of possible safety hazards, the number of accidents on the job can be reduced.

Careless use of office equipment can cause accidents and injuries. For example, file cabinet drawers which are filled with papers can be so heavy that the entire cabinet could tip over from the weight of one open drawer.

The bottom drawers of desks and file cabinets should never be left open since employees can easily trip over open drawers and injure themselves.

When reaching for objects on a high shelf, an employee should use a strong, sturdy object such as a stepstool to stand on. Makeshift platforms made out of books, papers, or boxes can easily collapse. Even chairs can slide out from under foot, causing serious injury.

Even at an employee's desk, safety hazards can occur. Frayed or cut wires should be repaired or replaced immediately. Computers which are not firmly anchored to the desk or table could fall, causing injury.

Smoking is one of the major causes of fires in the office. A lighted match or improperly extinguished cigarette thrown into a wastebasket filled with paper could cause a major fire with possible loss of life. Where smoking is permitted, ashtrays should be used. Smoking is particularly dangerous in offices were flammable chemicals are used.

5. The goal of an effective safety program is to
   A. reduce office accidents
   B. stop employees from smoking on the job
   C. encourage employees to continue their education
   D. eliminate high shelves in offices

6. Desks and file cabinets can become safety hazards when
   A. their drawers are left open
   B. they are used as wastebaskets
   C. they are makeshift
   D. they are not anchored securely to the floor

7. Smoking is especially hazardous when it occurs
   A. near exposed wires
   B. in a crowded office
   C. in an area where flammable chemicals are used
   D. where books and papers are stored

8. Accidents are likely to occur when
   A. employees' desks are cluttered with books and papers
   B. employees are not aware of safety hazards
   C. employees close desk drawers
   D. stepstools are used to reach high objects

9. Assume that part of your job as a worker in the accounting division of a city agency is to answer the telephone.
   When you first answer the telephone, it is LEAST important to tell the caller
   A. your title
   B. your name
   C. the name of your unit
   D. the name of your agency

10. Assume that you are assigned to work as a receptionist, and your duties are to answer phones, greet visitors, and do other general office work. You are busy with a routine job when several visitors approach your desk.
    The BEST action to take is to
    A. ask the visitors to have a seat and assist them after your work is completed
    B. tell the visitors that you are busy and they should return at a more convenient time
    C. stop working long enough to assist the visitors
    D. continue working and wait for the visitors to ask you for assistance

11. Assume that your supervisor has chosen you to take a special course during hours to learn a new payroll procedure. Although you know that you were chosen because of your good work record, a co-worker, who feels that he should have been chosen, has been telling everyone in your unit that the choice was unfair.
    Of the following, the BEST way to handle this situation FIRST is to
    A. suggest to the co-worker that everything in life is unfair
    B. contact your union representative in case your co-worker presents a formal grievance
    C. tell your supervisor about your co-worker's complaints and let her handle the situation
    D. tell the co-worker that you were chosen because of your superior work record

12. Assume that while you are working on an assignment which must be completed quickly, a supervisor from another unit asks you to obtain information for her.
    Of the following, the BEST way to respond to her request is to
    A. tell her to return in an hour since you are busy
    B. give her the names of some people in her own unit who could help her
    C. tell her you are busy and refer her to a co-worker
    D. tell her that you are busy and ask her if she could wait until you finish your assignment

13. A co-worker in your unit is often off from work because of illness. Your supervisor assigns the co-worker's work to you when she is not there. Lately, doing her work has interfered with your own job.
    The BEST action for you to take FIRST is to
    A. discuss the problem with your supervisor
    B. complete your own work before starting your co-worker's work
    C. ask other workers in your unit to assist you
    D. work late in order to get the jobs done

14. During the month of June, 40,587 people attended a city-owned swimming pool. In July, 13,014 more people attended the swimming pool than the number that had attended in June. In August, 39,655 people attended the swimming pool. The TOTAL number of people who attended the swimming pool during the months of June, July, and August was 14.____

    A. 80,242   B. 93,256   C. 133,843   D. 210,382

Questions 15-22.

DIRECTIONS: Questions 15 through 22 test how well you understand what you read. It will be necessary for you to read carefully because your answers to these questions must be based ONLY on the information in the following paragraphs.

    The telephone directory is made up of two books. The first book consists of the introductory section and the alphabetical listing of names section. The second book is the classified directory (also known as the yellow pages). Many people who are familiar with one book do not realize how useful the other can be. The efficient office worker should become familiar with both books in order to make the best use of this important source of information.

    The introductory section gives general instructions for finding numbers in the alphabetical listing and classified directory. This section also explains how to use the telephone company's many services, including the operator and information services, gives examples of charges for local and long-distance calls, and lists area codes for the entire country. In addition, this section provides a useful zip code map.

    The alphabetical listing of names section lists the names, addresses, and telephone numbers of subscribers in an area. Guide names, or *telltales*, are on the top corner of each page. These guide names indicate the first and last name to be found on that page. *Telltales* help locate any particular name quickly. A cross-reference spelling is also given to help locate names which are spelled several different ways. City, state, and federal government agencies are listed under the major government heading. For example, an agency of the federal government would be listed under *United States Government*.

    The classified directory, or yellow pages, is a separate book. In this section are advertising services, public transportation line maps, shopping guides, and listings of businesses arranged by the type of product or services they offer. This book is most useful when looking for the name or phone number of a business when all that is known is the type of product offered and the address, or when trying to locate a particular type of business in an area. Businesses listed in the classified directory can usually be found in the alphabetical listing of names section. When the name of the business is known, you will find the address or phone number more quickly in the alphabetical listing of names section.

15. The introductory section provides 15.____
    A. shopping guides   B. government listings
    C. business listings   D. information services

16. Advertising services would be found in the 16.____
    A. introductory section   B. alphabetical listing of names section\
    C. classified directory   D. information services

5 (#3)

17. According to the information in the above passage for locating government agencies, the Information Office of the Department of Consumer Affairs of New York City government would be alphabetically listed FIRST under
    A. *I* for Information Offices
    B. *D* for Department of Consumer Affairs
    C. *N* for New York City
    D. *G* for government

17._____

18. When the name of a business is known, the QUICKEST way to find the phone number is to look in the
    A. classified directory
    B. introductory section
    C. alphabetical listing of name section
    D. advertising service section

18._____

19. The QUICKEST way to find the phone number of a business when the type of service a business offers and its address is known is to look in the
    A. classified directory
    B. alphabetical listing of names section
    C. introductory section
    D. information service

19._____

20. What is a *telltale*?
    A. An alphabetical listing
    B. A guide name
    C. A map
    D. A cross-reference listing

20._____

21. The BEST way to find a postal zip code is to look in the
    A. classified directory
    B. introductory section
    C. alphabetical listing of names section
    D. government heading

21._____

22. To help find names which have several different spellings, the telephone directory provides
    A. cross-reference spelling
    B. *telltales*
    C. spelling guides
    D. advertising services

22._____

23. Assume that your agency has been given $2,025 to purchase file cabinets. If each file cabinet costs $135, how many file cabinet can your agency purchase?
    A. 8   B. 10   C. 15   D. 16

23._____

24. Assume that your unit ordered 14 staplers at a total cost of $30.20 and each stapler cost the same.
    The cost of one stapler was MOST NEARLY
    A. $1.02   B. $1.61   C. $2.16   D. $2.26

24._____

25. Assume that you are responsible for counting and recording licensing fees collected by your department. On a particular day, your department collected in fees 40 checks in the amount of $6 each, 80 checks in the amount of $4 each, 45 twenty dollar bills, 30 ten dollar bills, 42 five dollar bills, and 186 one dollar bills.
The TOTAL amount in fees collected on that day was
    A. $1,406 B. $1,706 C. $2,156 D. $2,356

26. Assume that you are responsible for your agency's petty cash fund. During the month of February, you pay out 7 $2.00 subway fares and one taxi fare for $10.85. You pay out nothing else from the fund. At the end of February, you count the money left in the fund and find 3 one dollar bills, 4 quarters, 5 dimes, and 4 nickels.
The amount of money you had available in the petty cash fund at the BEGINNING of February was
    A. $4.70 B. $16.35 C. $24.85 D. $29.55

27. You overhear your supervisor criticize a co-worker for handling equipment in an unsafe way. You feel that the criticism may be unfair.
Of the following, it would be BEST for you to
    A. take your co-worker aside and tell her how you feel about your supervisor's comments
    B. interrupt the discussion and defend your co-worker to your supervisor
    C. continue working as if you had not overheard the discussion
    D. make a list of other workers who have violated safety rules and give it to your supervisor

28. Assume that you have been assigned to work on a long-term project with an employee who is known for being uncooperative.
In beginning to work with this employee, it would be LEAST desirable for you to
    A. understand why the person is uncooperative
    B. act in a calm manner rather than an emotional manner
    C. be appreciative of the co-worker's work
    D. report the co-worker's lack of cooperation to your supervisor

29. Assume that you are assigned to sell tickets at a city-owned ice skating rink. An adult ticket costs $4.50, and a children's ticket costs $2.25. At the end of a day, you find that you have sold 36 adult tickets and 80 children's tickets.
The TOTAL amount of money you collected for that day was
    A. $244.80 B. $318.00 C. $342.00 D. $348.00

30. If each office worker files 487 index cards in one hour, how many card can 26 office workers file in one hour?
    A. 10,662 B. 12,175 C. 12,662 D. 14,266

KEY (CORRECT ANSWERS)

1.	D	11.	C	21.	B
2.	B	12.	D	22.	A
3.	A	13.	A	23.	C
4.	D	14.	C	24.	C
5.	A	15.	D	25.	C
6.	A	16.	C	26.	D
7.	C	17.	C	27.	C
8.	B	18.	C	28.	D
9.	A	19.	A	29.	C
10.	C	20.	B	30.	C

RECORD KEEPING
EXAMINATION SECTION
TEST 1

DIRECTIONS: Each question or incomplete statement is followed by several suggested answers or completions. Select the one that BEST answers the question or completes the statement. *PRINT THE LETTER OF THE CORRECT ANSWER IN THE SPACE AT THE RIGHT.*

Questions 1-15.

DIRECTIONS: Questions 1 through 15 are to be answered on the basis of the following list of company names below. Arrange a file alphabetically, word-by-word, disregarding punctuation, conjunctions, and apostrophes. Then answer the questions.

    A Bee C Reading Materials
    ABCO Parts
    A Better Course for Test Preparation
    AAA Auto Parts Co.
    A-Z Auto Parts, Inc.
    Aabar Books
    Abbey, Joanne
    Boman-Sylvan Law Firm
    BMW Autowerks
    C Q Service Company
    Chappell-Murray, Inc.
    E&E Life Insurance
    Emcrisco
    Gigi Arts
    Gordon, Jon & Associates
    SOS Plumbing
    Schmidt, J.B. Co.

1. Which of these files should appear FIRST?   1.____
   A. ABCO Parts
   B. A Bee C Reading Materials
   C. A Better Course for Test Preparation
   D. AAA Auto Parts Co.

2. Which of these files should appear SECOND?   2.____
   A. A-Z Auto Parts, Inc.
   B. A Bee C Reading Materials
   C. A Better Course for Test Preparation
   D. AAA Auto Parts Co.

3. Which of these files should appear THIRD?
   A. ABCO Parts
   B. A Bee C Reading Materials
   C. Aabar Books
   D. AAA Auto Parts Co.

4. Which of these files should appear FOURTH?
   A. Aabar Books
   B. ABCO Parts
   C. Abbey, Joanne
   D. AAA Auto Parts Co.

5. Which of these files should appear LAST?
   A. Gordon, Jon & Associates
   B. Gigi Arts
   C. Schmidt, J.B. Co.
   D. SOS Plumbing

6. Which of these files should appear between A-Z Auto Parts, Inc. and Abbey, Joanne?
   A. A Bee C Reading Materials
   B. AAA Auto Parts Co.
   C. ABCO Parts
   D. A Better Course for Test Preparation

7. Which of these files should appear between ABCO Parts and Aabar Books?
   A. A Bee C Reading Materials
   B. Abbey, Joanne
   C. Aabar Books
   D. A-Z Auto Parts

8. Which of these files should appear between Abbey, Joanne and Boman-Sylvan Law Firm?
   A. A Better Course for Test Preparation
   B. BMW Autowerks
   C. Chappell-Murray, Inc.
   D. Aabar Books

9. Which of these files should appear between Abbey, Joanne and C Q Service?
   A. A-Z Auto Parts, Inc.
   B. BMW Autowerks
   C. Choices A and B
   D. Chappell-Murray, Inc.

10. Which of these files should appear between C Q Service Company and Emcrisco?
    A. Chappell-Murray, Inc.
    B. E&E Life Insurance
    C. Gigi Arts
    D. Choices A and B

11. Which of these files should NOT appear between C Q Service Company and E&E Life Insurance?
    A. Gordon, Jon & Associates
    B. Emcrisco
    C. Gigi Arts
    D. All of the above

12. Which of these files should appear between Chappell-Murray, Inc. and Gigi Arts? 12.____
    A. C Q Service Inc., E&E Life Insurance, and Emcrisco
    B. Emcrisco, E&E Life Insurance, and Gordon, Jon & Associates
    C. E&E Life Insurance, and Emcrisco
    D. Emcrisco and Gordon, Jon & Associates

13. Which of these files should appear between Gordon, Jon & Associates and SOS Plumbing? 13.____
    A. Gigi Arts
    B. Schmidt, J.B. Co.
    C. Choices A and B
    D. None of the above

14. Each of the choices lists the four files in their proper alphabetical order EXCEPT 14.____
    A. E&E Life Insurance; Gigi Arts; Gordon, Jon & Associates; SOS Plumbing
    B. E&E Life Insurance; Emcrisco; Gigi Arts; SOS Plumbing
    C. Emcrisco; Gordon, Jon & Associates; SOS Plumbing; Schmidt, J.B. Co.
    D. Emcrisco; Gigi Arts; Gordon, Jon & Associates; SOS Plumbing

15. Which of the choices lists the four files in their proper alphabetical order? 15.____
    A. Gigi Arts; Gordon, Jon & Associates; SOS Plumbing; Schmidt, J.B. Co.
    B. Gordon, Jon & Associates; Gigi Arts; Schmidt, J.B. Co.; SOS Plumbing
    C. Gordon, Jon & Associates; Gigi Arts; SOS Plumbing; Schmidt, J.B. Co.
    D. Gigi Arts; Gordon, Jon & Associates; Schmidt, J.B. Co.; SOS Plumbing

16. The alphabetical filing order of two businesses with identical names is determined by the 16.____
    A. length of time each business has been operating
    B. addresses of the businesses
    C. last name of the company president
    D. no one of the above

17. In an alphabetical filing system, if a business name includes a number, it should be 17.____
    A. disregarded
    B. considered a number and placed at the end of an alphabetical section
    C. treated as though it were written in words and alphabetized accordingly
    D. considered a number and placed at the beginning of an alphabetical section

18. If a business name includes a contraction (such as *don't* or *it's*), how should that word be treated in an alphabetical system? 18.____
    A. Divide the word into its separate parts and treat it as two words
    B. Ignore the letters that come after the apostrophe
    C. Ignore the word that contains the contraction
    D. Ignore the apostrophe and consider all letters in the contraction

19. In what order should the parts of an address be considered when using an alphabetical filing system? 19._____
    A. City or town; state; street name; house or building number
    B. State; city or town; street name; house or building number
    C. House or building number; street name; city or town; state
    D. Street name; city or town; state

20. A business record should be cross-referenced when a(n) 20._____
    A. organization is known by an abbreviated name
    B. business has a name change because of a sale, incorporation, or other reason
    C. business is known by a *coined* or common name which differs from a dictionary spelling
    D. all of the above

21. A geographical filing system is MOST effective when 21._____
    A. location is more important than name
    B. many names or titles sound alike
    C. dealing with companies who have offices all over the world
    D. filing personal and business files

Questions 22-25.

DIRECTIONS: Questions 22 through 25 are to be answered on the basis of the list of items below, which are to be filed geographically. Organize the items geographically and then answer the questions.

    I. University Press at Berkeley, U.S.
    II. Maria Sanchez, Mexico City, Mexico
    III. Great Expectations Ltd. in London, England
    IV. Justice League, Cape Town, South Africa, Africa
    V. Crown Pearls Ltd. in London, England
    VI. Joseph Prasad in London, England

22. Which of the following arrangements of the items is composed according to the policy of: *Continent, Country, City, Firm or Individual Name*? 22._____
    A. V, III, IV, VI, II, I   B. IV, V, III, VI, II, I
    C. I, IV, V, III, VI, II   D. IV, V, III, VI, I, II

23. Which of the following files is arranged according to the policy of: 23._____
    Continent, Country, City, Firm or Individual Name?
    A. South Africa; Africa; Cape Town; Justice League
    B. Mexico; Mexico City; Maria Sanchez
    C. North America; United States; Berkeley; University Press
    D. England; Europe; London; Prasad, Joseph

24. Which of the following arrangements of the items is composed according to the   24.____
    policy of: *Country, City, Firm or Individual Name*?
    A. V, VI, III, II, IV, I   B. I, V, VI, III, II, IV
    C. VI, V, III, II, IV, I   D. V, III, VI, II, IV, I

25. Which of the following files is arranged according to a policy of: *Country,*   25.____
    City, Firm or Individual Name?
    A. England; London; Crown Pearls Ltd.
    B. North America; United States; Berkeley; University Press
    C. Africa; Cape Town; Justice League
    D. Mexico City; Mexico; Maria Sanchez

26. Under which of the following circumstances would a phonetic filing system be   26.____
    MOST effective?
    A. When the person in charge of filing can't spell very well
    B. With large files with names that sound alike
    C. With large files with names that are spelled alike
    D. All of the above

Questions 27-29.

DIRECTIONS: Questions 27 through 29 are to be answered on the basis of the following list of numerical files.

    I.   391-023-100
    II. 361-132-170
    III. 385-732-200
    IV. 381-432-150
    V.   391-632-387
    VI. 361-423-303
    VII. 391-123-271

27. Which of the following arrangements of the files follows a consecutive-digit   27.____
    system?
    A. II, III, IV, I   B. I, V, VII, III   C. II, IV, III, I   D. III, I, V, VII

28. Which of the following arrangements follows a terminal-digit system?   28.____
    A. I, VII, II, IV, III   B. II, I, IV, V, VII
    C. VII, VI, V, IV, III   D. I, IV, II, III, VII

29. Which of the following lists follows a middle-digit system?   29.____
    A. I, VII, II, VI, IV, V, III   B. I, II, VII, IV, VI, V, III
    C. VII, II, I, III, V, VI, IV   D. VII, I, II, IV, VI, V, III

Questions 30-31.

DIRECTIONS: Questions 30 and 31 are to be answered on the basis of the following information.

  I. Reconfirm Laura Bates appointment with James Caldecort on December 12 at 9:30 A.M.
  II. Laurence Kinder contact Julia Lucas on August 3 and set up a meeting for week of September 23 at 4 P.M.
  III. John Lutz contact Larry Waverly on August 3 and set up appointment for September 23 at 9:30 A.M.
  IV. Call for tickets for Gerry Stanton August 21 for New Jersey on September 23, flight 143 at 4:43 P.M.

30. A chronological file for the above information would be 30._____
    A. IV, III, II, I   B. III, II, IV, I   C. IV, II, III, I   D. III, I, II, IV

31. Using the above information, a chronological file for the date September 23 would be 31._____
    A. II, III, IV   B. III, I, IV   C. III, II, IV   D. IV, III, II

Questions 32-34.

DIRECTIONS: Questions 32 through 34 are to be answered on the basis of the following information.

  I. Call Roger Epstein, Ashoke Naipaul, Jon Anderson, and Sara Washingon on April 19 at 1:00 P.M. to set up meeting with Alika D'Ornay for June 6 in New York.
  II. Call Martin Ames before noon on April 19 to confirm afternoon meeting with Bob Greenwood on April 20th.
  III. Set up meeting room at noon for 2:30 P.M. meeting on April 19th.
  IV. Ashley Stanton contact Bob Greenwood at 9:00 A.M. on April 20 and set up meeting for June 6 at 8:30 A.M.
  V. Carol Guiland contact Shelby Van Ness during afternoon of April 20 and set up meeting for June 6 at 10:00 A.M.
  VI. Call airline and reserve tickets on June 6 for Roger Epstein trip to Denver on July 8.
  VII. Meeting at 2:30 P.M. on April 19th.

32. A chronological file for all of the above information would be 32._____
    A. II, I, III, VII, V, IV, VI   B. III, VII, II, I, IV, V, VI
    C. III, VII, I, II, V, IV, VI   D. II, III, I, VII, IV, V, VI

33. A chronological file for the date of April 19th would be 33._____
    A. II, III, VII, I   B. II, III, I, VII   C. VII, I, III, II   D. III, VII, I, II

34. Add the following information to the file, and then create a chronological file for April 20th: VIII. April 20: 3:00 P.M. meeting between Bob Greenwood and Martin Ames.
    A. IV, V, VIII   B. IV, VIII, V   C. VIII, V, IV   D. V, IV, VIII

35. The PRIMARY advantage of computer records over a manual system is
    A. speed of retrieval   B. accuracy
    C. cost   D. potential file loss

KEY (CORRECT ANSWERS)

1.	B	11.	D	21.	A	31.	C
2.	C	12.	C	22.	B	32.	D
3.	D	13.	B	23.	C	33.	B
4.	A	14.	C	24.	D	34.	A
5.	D	15.	D	25.	A	35.	A
6.	C	16.	B	26.	B		
7.	B	17.	C	27.	C		
8.	B	18.	D	28.	D		
9.	C	19.	A	29.	A		
10.	D	20.	D	30.	B		

EXAMINATION SECTION
TEST 1

DIRECTIONS: Each question or incomplete statement is followed by several suggested answers or completions. Select the one that BEST answers the question or completes the statement. *PRINT THE LETTER OF THE CORRECT ANSWER IN THE SPACE AT THE RIGHT.*

1. Which of the following is the acceptable format for typing the date line?   1.____
   - A. 12/2/16
   - B. December 2, 2016
   - C. December 2nd, 2016
   - D. Dec. 2 2016

2. When typing a letter, which of the following is INACCURATE?   2.____
   - A. If the letter is to be more than one page long, subsequent sheets should be blank, but should match the letterhead sheet in size, color, weight, and texture.
   - B. Long quoted material must be centered and single-spaced internally.
   - C. Quotation marks must be used when there is long quoted material.
   - D. Double spacing is used above and below tables and long quotations to set them off from the rest of the material.

3. Which of the following is INACCURATE?   3.____
   - A. When an addressee's title in an inside address would overrun the center of a page, it's best to carry part of the title over to another line and to indent it by two spaces.
   - B. It is permissible to use ordinal numbers in an inside address.
   - C. In addresses involving street numbers under three, the number is written out in full.
   - D. In the inside address, suite, apartment or room numbers should be placed on the line after the street address.

4. All of the following are common styles of business letters EXCEPT   4.____
   - A. simplified
   - B. block
   - C. direct
   - D. executive

5. Please select the two choices below that correctly represent how a continuation sheet heading may be typed.   5.____
   - I. Page 2
      Mr. Alan Post
      June 25, 2016
   - II. Page 2
      Mr. Alan Post
      6-25-16
   - III. Mr. Alan Post   -2-
         June 25, 2016
   - IV. Mr. Alan Post   -2-
         6-25-16

   The CORRECT answer is:
   - A. I, II
   - B. II, III
   - C. I, III
   - D. II, IV

6. Which of the following is INCORRECT? It is   6.____
   - A. permissible to abbreviate honorifics in the inside address
   - B. permissible to abbreviate company or organizational names, departmental designations, or organizational titles in the inside address

C. permissible to use abbreviations in the inside address if they have been used on the printed letterhead and form part of the official company name
D. sometimes permissible to omit the colon after the salutation

7. Which of the following is INCORRECT? 7.____

   A. The subject line of a letter gives the main idea of the message as succinctly as possible.
   B. If a letter contains an enclosure, there should be a notation indicating this.
   C. Important enclosures ought to be listed numerically and described.
   D. An enclosure notation should be typed flush with the right margin.

8. Which of the following is INACCURATE about inside addresses? 8.____

   A. An intraoffice or intracompany mail stop number such as DA 3C 61B is put after the organization or company name with at least two spaces intervening.
   B. Words such as *Avenue* should not be abbreviated.
   C. With the exception of runovers, the inside address should not be more than five full lines.
   D. The inside address includes the recipient's courtesy or honorific title and his or her full name on line one; the recipient's title on the next line; the recipient's official organizational affiliation on the next line; the street address on the penultimate line; and the city, state, and zip code on the last line.

9. Which of the following is an INCORRECT example of how to copy recipients when using copy notation? 9.____

   A. cc: Martin A.Sheen
   B. cc: Ms. Connors
          Ms. Grogan
          Ms. Reynolds
   C. CC: Martin A. Sheen
   D. cc: Mr. Right
          Mr. Wrong
          Mr. Perfect

10. When typing a memo, all of the following are true EXCEPT 10.____

    A. it is permissible to use an abbreviation like 1/1/16
    B. the subject line should be underlined
    C. titles such as *Mr.* or *Dr.* are usually not used on the *To* line
    D. unless the memo is very short, paragraphs should be single-spaced and double spacing should be used to separate the paragraphs from each other

11. When typing a letter, which of the following is INACCURATE? 11.____

    A. Paragraphs in business letters are usually single-spaced, with double spacing separating them from each other.
    B. Margin settings used on subsequent sheets should match those used on the letterhead sheet.
    C. If the message contains an enumerated list, it is best to block and center the listed material by five or six more spaces, right and left.
    D. A quotation of more than three typed lines must be single-spaced and centered on the page.

12. A letter that is to be signed by Hazel Alice Putney, but written by Mary Jane Roberts, and typed by Alice Carol Bell would CORRECTLY bear the following set of initials:

    A. HAP:MJR:acb
    B. HAP:MJR:ab
    C. HAP:mjr:acb
    D. HAP:mjr:ab

13. Which of the following is INCORRECT?

    A. My dear Dr. Jones:
    B. Dear Accounting Department:
    C. Dear Dr. Jones:
    D. Dear Mr. Al Lee, Esq.:

14. Which of the following is INCORRECT?

    A. Bcc stands for blind copy or blind courtesy copy.
    B. When a blind copy is used, the notation bcc appears only on the original.
    C. When a blind copy is used, the notation may appear in the top left corner of the letterhead sheet.
    D. If following a letter style that uses indented paragraphs, the postscript should be indented in exactly the same manner.

15. All of the following are true of the complimentary close EXCEPT

    A. it is typed two lines beneath the last line of the message
    B. when using a minimal punctuation system, you may omit the comma in the complimentary close if you have used a colon in the salutation
    C. where the complimentary close is placed may vary
    D. the first word of the complimentary close is capitalized

16. When typing a letter, which of the following is INACCURATE?

    A. Tables should be centered.
    B. If the letter is to be more than one page long, at least three lines of the message itself should be carried over.
    C. The message begins two lines below the salutation in almost all letter styles.
    D. Triple spacing should be used above and below lists to set them off from the rest of the letter.

17. Which one of the following is INCORRECT?

    A. When used, special mailing instructions should be indicated on both the envelope and the letter itself.
    B. Depending upon the length of the message and the available space, special mailing instructions are usually typed flush left, about four spaces below the date line and about two lines above the first line of the inside address.
    C. Certification, registration, special delivery, and overseas air mail are all considered special mailing instructions.
    D. Special mailing instructions should not be typed in capital letters.

18. Which of the following is INCORRECT?

    A. When a letter is intended to be personal or confidential, these instructions are typewritten in capital letters on the envelope and on the letter itself.

B. When a letter is intended to be personal or confidential, these instructions are typewritten in capital letters on the envelope, but not on the letter.
C. A letter marked PERSONAL is an eyes-only communication for the recipient.
D. A letter marked CONFIDENTIAL means that the recipient and any other authorized person may open and read it.

19. All of the following are true in regard to copy notation EXCEPT

    A. when included in a letter, a copy notation should be typed flush with the left margin, two lines below the signature block or two lines below any preceding notation
    B. copy notation should appear after writer/typist initials and/or enclosure notations, if these are used
    C. the copy recipient's full name and address should be indicated
    D. if more than one individual is to be copied, recipients should be listed in alphabetical order according to full name or initials

20. When addressing envelopes, which of the following is INACCURATE?

    A. When both street address and box number are used, the destination of the letter should be placed on the line just above the city, state, and zip code line.
    B. Special mailing instructions are typed in capital letters below the postage.
    C. Special handling instructions should be typed in capital letters and underlined.
    D. The address should be single-spaced.

21. All of the following should be capitalized EXCEPT the

    A. first word of a direct quotation
    B. first word in the continuation of a split, single-sentence quotation
    C. names of organizations
    D. names of places and geographic districts, regions, divisions, and locales

22. All of the following are true about capitalization EXCEPT

    A. words indicating direction and regions are capitalized
    B. the names of rivers, seas, lakes, mountains, and oceans are capitalized
    C. the names of nationalities, tribes, languages, and races are capitalized
    D. civil, military, corporate, royal and noble, honorary, and religious titles are capitalized when they precede a name

23. All of the following are true about capitalization EXCEPT

    A. key words in the titles of musical, dramatic, artistic, and literary works are capitalized as are the first and last words
    B. the first word of the salutation and of the complimentary close of a letter is capitalized
    C. abbreviations and acronyms are not capitalized
    D. the days of the week, months of the year, holidays, and holy days are capitalized

24. All of the following are true EXCEPT

    A. an apostrophe indicates the omission of letters in contractions
    B. an apostrophe indicates the possessive case of singular and plural nouns

C. an apostrophe should not be used to indicate the omission of figures in dates
D. ellipses are used to indicate the omission of words or sentences within quoted material

25. All of the following are true EXCEPT

    A. brackets may be used to enclose words or passages in quotations to indicate the insertion of material written by someone other than the original writer
    B. brackets may be used to enclose material that is inserted within material already in parentheses
    C. a dash, rather than a colon, should be used to introduce a list
    D. a colon may be used to introduce a long quotation

26. All of the following are true EXCEPT a(n)

    A. comma may be used to set off short quotations and sayings
    B. apostrophe is often used to represent the word *per*
    C. dash may be used to indicate a sudden change or break in continuity
    D. dash may be used to set apart an emphatic or defining phrase

27. All of the following are true EXCEPT

    A. a hyphen may be used as a substitute for the word *to* between figures or words
    B. parentheses are used to enclose material that is not an essential part of the sentence and that, if not included, would not change its meaning
    C. single quotation marks are used to enclose quotations within quotations
    D. semicolons and colons are put inside closing quotation marks

28. All of the following are true EXCEPT

    A. commas and periods should be put inside closing quotation marks
    B. for dramatic effect, a semicolon may be used instead of a comma to signal longer pauses
    C. a semicolon is used to set off city and state in geographic names
    D. italics are used to represent the titles of magazines and newspapers

29. According to standard rules for typing, two spaces are left after a

    A. closing parenthesis   B. comma
    C. number   D. colon

30. All of the following are true EXCEPT

    A. rounding out large numbers is often acceptable
    B. it is best to use numerical figures to express specific hours, measures, dates, page numbers, coordinates, and addresses
    C. when a sentence begins with a number, it is best to use numerical figures rather than to spell the number out
    D. when two or more numbers appear in one sentence, it is best to spell them out consistently or use numerical figures consistently, regardless of the size of the numbers

31. All of the following are true about word division EXCEPT
    A. words should not be divided on a single letter
    B. it is acceptable to carry over two-letter endings
    C. the final word in a paragraph should not be divided
    D. words in headings should not be divided

32. All of the following are true of word division EXCEPT
    A. it is preferable to divide words of three or more syllables after the consonant
    B. it is best to avoid breaking words on more than two consecutive lines
    C. words should be divided according to pronunciation
    D. two-syllable words are divided at the end of the first syllable

33. All of the following are true of word division EXCEPT
    A. words with short prefixes should be divided after the prefix
    B. prefixes and combining forms of more than one syllable should be divided after the first syllable
    C. the following word endings are not divided: -gion, -gious, -sial, -sion, -tial, -tion, -tious, -ceous, -cial, -cient, -cion, -cious, and -geous
    D. words ending in -er should not be divided if the division could only occur on the -er form

34. All of the following are true about word division EXCEPT
    A. words should be divided so that the part of the word left at the end of the line will suggest the word
    B. abbreviations should not be divided
    C. the suffixes -able and -ible are usually divided instead of being carried over intact to the next line
    D. when the addition of -ed, -est, -er, or a similar ending causes the doubling of a final consonant, the added consonant is carried over

35. All of the following are true of word division EXCEPT
    A. words with doubled consonants are usually divided between those consonants
    B. it is permissible to divide contractions
    C. words of one syllable should not be split
    D. it is best to try to avoid divisions that add a hyphen to an already hyphenated word

36. All of the following are true of word division EXCEPT
    A. dividing proper names should be avoided wherever possible
    B. two consonants, preceded and followed by a vowel, are divided after the first consonant
    C. even though two adjoining vowels are sounded separately, it is best not to divide between the two vowels
    D. it is best not to divide the month and day when typing dates, but the year may be carried over to the next line

37. Which of the following four statements are CORRECT? It would be acceptable to divide the word
    I. *organization* after the first *a* in the word
    II. *recommend* after the first *m*
    III. *interface* between the *r* and the *f*
    IV. *development* between the *e* and the *l*
    The CORRECT answer is:

    A. I *only*
    B. II, III
    C. II *only*
    D. I, II, III

38. Which of the following is divided INCORRECTLY?

    A. usu-ally
    B. call-ing
    C. pro-blem
    D. micro-computer

39. Which of the following is divided INCORRECTLY?

    A. imag-inary
    B. commun-ity
    C. manage-able
    D. commun-ion

40. Which of the following is divided INCORRECTLY?

    A. spa-ghetti
    B. retro-spective
    C. proof-reader
    D. fix-ed

41. Which of the following is divided INCORRECTLY?

    A. Mr. Han-rahan
    B. control-lable
    C. pro-jectile
    D. proj-ect

42. Which of the following is divided INCORRECTLY?

    A. prom-ise
    B. han-dling
    C. have-n't
    D. pro-duce

43. Which of the following is divided INCORRECTLY?

    A. ship-ped
    B. audi-ble
    C. hypo-crite
    D. refer-ring

44. Which of the following is divided INCORRECTLY?

    A. particu-lar
    B. spac-ious
    C. chang-ing
    D. capac-ity

45. There is a critical need to develop the ability to control the mind, especailly the ability to stop repeating negative thoughts. Often, when we must swallow our anger, we are left running an enless tape of thoughts. We can't stop thinking about what the person said and what we should have said in response. To combat this tendency, it is helpful to practice witnessing our thoughts. If we can remain detached from them, we won't fuel them, and they will just run out of gas. As we watch them, we also learn a lot about ourselves. The catch here is not to judge them. Judging may lead to selfblaming, blaming others, excuses, rationalizations, and other thoughts that just add fuel. Another technique is is substituting positive thoughts for negative ones.

8 (#1)

It is difficult to do this in the "heat of the moment". With practice, however, its possible to train the mind to do what we want it to do and to contain what we want it to contain. A mind is like a garden – we can weed it, or we can let it grow wild.
The above paragraph contains a number of typographical errors.
How many lines in this paragraph contain typographical errors?

A. 5   B. 6   C. 8   D. 9

KEY (CORRECT ANSWERS)

1. B	11. D	21. B	31. B	41. A
2. C	12. A	22. A	32. A	42. A
3. D	13. D	23. C	33. B	43. A
4. C	14. B	24. C	34. C	44. B
5. C	15. B	25. C	35. B	45. C
6. B	16. D	26. B	36. C	
7. D	17. D	27. D	37. B	
8. B	18. B	28. C	38. C	
9. D	19. C	29. D	39. B	
10. B	20. C	30. C	40. D	

TEST 2

DIRECTIONS: Each sentence may or may not contain problems in capitalization or punctuation. If there is an error, select the number of the underlined part that must be changed to make the sentence correct. If the sentence has no error, select choice E. No sentence contains more than one error.

1. Is the choice for <u>P</u>resident of the company<u> George Dawson</u><u> </u> or Marilyn Kappel<u> ?</u> <u>No error</u>
                   A   B   C   D   E

2. "To tell you the truth<u> ,</u> I was really <u>disappointed</u> that our <u>F</u>all percentages did not show more sales growth<u> ,</u> " remarked the bookkeeper. <u>No error</u>
        A   B   C   D   E

3. Bruce gave his <u>U</u>ncle clear directions to go <u>s</u>outh on Maplewood Drive<u> ,</u> turn left at the intersection with Birch Lane, and then proceed for two miles until he reached Columbia <u>C</u>ounty . <u>No error</u>
                  A   B   C

4. Janet hopes to transfer to a <u>c</u>ollege in the <u>e</u>ast <u>d</u>uring her <u>j</u>unior year. <u>No error</u>
                                      A   B C   D   E

5. The <u>D</u>eclaration <u>o</u>f Independence states<u> </u> that we have the right to the pursuit of <u>H</u>appiness , but it doesn't guarantee that we'll ever find it. <u>No error</u>

6. We campaigned hard for the <u>m</u>ayor<u>,</u> but we<u>'</u>re still not sure if he'll win against <u>S</u>enator Frankovich. <u>No error</u>

7. Mr. <u>Butler'</u>s <u>F</u>ord was parked right behind <u>our's</u> on Atlantic <u>A</u>venue . <u>No error</u>
            A B   C   D   E

8. "I respect your <u>opinion,</u> but I cannot agree with <u>it."</u> commented my <u>g</u>randmother. <u>No error</u>
     A   B   C   D   E

9. My friends, of course, were surprised when when I did so well on the Math section
      A   B   C   D
of the test. No error
             E

10. Dr. Vogel and Senator Rydell decided that the meeting would be held on February 6,
                  A   B   C
in Ithaca, New York. No error
   D   E

11. "Frank, do you understand what we're telling you?" asked the doctor. No error
        A   B   C   D   E

12. When I asked my daughter what she knew about politics, she claimed she
                    A   B   C
knew nothing. No error
         D   E

13. "If you went to my high school, dad, you'd see things differently," snapped Sean.
                     A   A   B   C   D
No error
    E

14. In Carlos' third year of high school, he took geometry, psychology, french, and chemis-
       A   B   B   C   D
try. No error
       E

15. "When you enter the building," the guard instructed us, "turn left down the long, wind-
                              A   B   C   D
ing corridor." No error
                  E

16. We hope to spend a weekend in the Catskill Mountains in the spring, and we'd like to
                                                A   B   C   D
go to Florida in January. No error
                           E

17. A clerk in the department of Justice asked Carol and me if we were there on business or
     A   B   C
just sight-seeing. No error
              D   E

18. Jamie joined a cult, Harry's in a rock band, and Carol-Ann is studying chinese literature
       A   B   C
    at the University of Southern California. No error
            D   E

19. Parker Flash asked if my band had ever played at the
                    A
    Purple Turnip, a club in Orinoco Hills. No error
       B   C   D   E

20. "The gift of the Magi" is a short story by O'Henry that deals with the sad ironies of life.
         A   B C   D
    No error
       E

21. Darwin's theory was developed, as a result of his trip to the Galapagos Islands..
         A B   C   D
    No error
       E

22. Is 10 Downing street the address of Sherlock Holmes or the British Prime Minister?
            A   B   C   D
    No error
       E

23. While President Johnson was in Office, his Great Society program passed a great deal
             A   B   C   D
    of important legislation. No error
                               E

24. If, as the American Industrial Health Council's study says, one out of every five can-
        A   B   C
    cers today is caused by the workplace, it is a tragic indictment of what is happening
                                 D
    there. No error
             E

25. According to the Articles of Confederation, Congress could issue money, but it could
                                A   B   C
    not prevent States from issuing their own money. No error
              D   E

26. "I'd really like to know whos going to be shoveling the driveway this winter," said
    　　　　　　　　　　 A　B　　　　　　　　　　　　　　　　　　　　　　　　C　　D

    Laverne. No error
    　　　　　　 E

27. According to Carl Jung the Swiss psychologist, playing with fantasy is the key to cre-
    　　　　　　　　　　A　　B　　　　　　　　C　　　　　　　　　　　　　　D

    ativity. No error
    　　　　　　 E

28. Don't you find it odd that people would prefer jumping A off the Golden Gate bridge to
    　　 A　　　　　　　　　　　　　　　　　　　　　　　　　　　　　　　　　　　　B

    jumping off other bridges in the area ? No error
    　　　　　　　　　　　　　 C　　D　　 E

29. While driving through the South, we saw many of the sites of famous Civil war battles. .
    　　　　　　　　　　　　A　　B　　　　　　　　　　　　　　　　　　　　C　　D

    No error
    　 E

30. Although I have always valued my Grandmother's china, I prefer her collection
    　　　　　　　　　　　　　　　　　　　A　　　　　　　　B　C

    of South American art. No error
    　　D　　　　　　　　 E

KEY (CORRECT ANSWERS)

1.	A		16.	E
2.	C		17.	B
3.	A		18.	C
4.	B		19.	C
5.	D		20.	A
6.	E		21.	C
7.	C		22.	B
8.	E		23.	B
9.	D		24.	D
10.	E		25.	D
11.	A		26.	B
12.	B		27.	A
13.	C		28.	B
14.	D		29.	C
15.	E		30.	A

EXAMINATION SECTION

TEST 1

DIRECTIONS: Each question or incomplete statement is followed by several suggested answers or completions. Select the one that BEST answers the question or completes the statement. *PRINT THE LETTER OF THE CORRECT ANSWER IN THE SPACE AT THE RIGHT.*

1. The ʌ or caret symbol is a proofreader's mark which means that a
    A. space should have been left between two words
    B. new paragraph should be indicated
    C. word, phrase, or punctuation mark should be inserted
    D. word that is abbreviated should be spelled out

2. Of the following items, the one which should NOT be omitted from a typed inter-office memorandum is the
    A. salutation
    B. complementary closing
    C. formal signature
    D. names of those to receive copies

3. A typed rough draft should be double-spaced and should have wide margins PRIMARILY in order to
    A. save time in making typing corrections
    B. provide room for making insertions and corrections
    C. insure that the report is well-organized
    D. permit faster typing of the draft

4. In tabular reports, when a main heading, secondary heading, and single line of columnar headings are used, a triple space (2 blank lines) would be used after the _____ heading(s).
    A. main
    B. secondary
    C. columnar
    D. main and secondary

5. You have been requested to type a letter to Mr. Brown, a district attorney of a small town.
    Of the following, the CORRECT salutation to use is Dear
    A. District Attorney Brown:
    B. Mr. District Attorney:
    C. Mr. Brown:
    D. Honorable Brown:

6. A form letter that is sent to the public can be made to look more personal in appearance by doing all of the following EXCEPT
    A. using a meter stamp on the envelope of the letter
    B. having the letter signed with pen and ink
    C. using a good quality of paper for the letter
    D. matching the type used in the letter with that used for fill-ins

7. A senior typist opens a word-processing application to instruct a typist to create a table that contains three column headings. Under each column heading are three items.
Of the following, which sequence should the senior typist tell the typist to use when creating this table?
   A. First type the headings, and then type the items under them, a column at a time
   B. type each heading with its column of items under it, one column at a time
   C. first type the column of items, then center the headings above them
   D. type the headings and items across the page line by line

7.____

8. When a letter is addressed to an agency and a particular person should see it, an *attention line* is used.
This attention line is USUALLY found
   A. on the envelope only
   B. above the address
   C. below the address
   D. after the agency named in the address

8.____

9. The typing technique of *justifying* is used to
   A. decide how wide margins of different sized letters should be
   B. make all the lines of copy end evenly on the right-hand margin
   C. center headings above columns on tabular typed material
   D. condense the amount of space that is needed to make a manuscript look presentable

9.____

10. The date line on a letter is typed correctly when the date is ALL on one line
    A. with the month written out
    B. with slashes between the numbers
    C. and the month is abbreviated
    D. with a period at the end

10.____

11. When considering how wide to make a column when typing a table, the BASIC rule to follow is that the column should be as wide as the longest
    A. item in the body of the column
    B. heading of all of the columns
    C. item in the body or heading of that column
    D. heading or the longest item in the body of any column on that page

11.____

12. When a lengthy quotation is included in a letter or a report, it must be indicated that it is quoted material. This may be done by
    A. enclosing the quotation in parentheses
    B. placing an exclamation point at the end of the quotation
    C. using the apostrophe marks
    D. indenting from the regular margins on the left and right

12.____

13. In order to reach the highest rate of speed and the greatest degree of accuracy while typing, it is LEAST important to
    A. maintain good posture
    B. keep the hands and arms at a comfortable level
    C. strike the keys evenly
    D. keep the typing action in the wrists

13.____

14. It has been shown that the rate of typing and dictation drops when the secretary is not familiar with the language or topic of the copy.
    A practice that a supervisor might BEST advise to improve the knowledge and therefore increase the rate of typing dictation for such material would be for the secretary to
    A. plan a conference with her supervisor to discuss the subject matter
    B. read and review correspondence and related technical journals that come into the office
    C. recopy or retype previously transcribed material as practice
    D. withdraw sample materials from the files to take home for study

14.____

15. The one of the following in which the tab key is NOT generally used is the
    A. placement of the complimentary close and signature line
    B. indentation of paragraphs
    C. placement of the date line
    D. centering of title headings

15.____

16. In order for a business letter to be effective, it is LEAST important that it
    A. say what is meant simply and directly
    B. be written in formal language
    C. include all information the receiver needs to know
    D. be courteously written

16.____

17. If you are momentarily called away from your desk while typing a report of a confidential nature, you should cover or turn the copy over and
    A. remove the page being typed from the computer and file the report
    B. ask someone to watch your desk for you
    C. close the document so that the page is not visible
    D. spread a folder over the computer screen to conceal it

17.____

18. When typing a table that contains a column of figures and a column of words, the PROPER alignment of the column of figures and the column of words should be an even _____ the column of words.
    A. right-hand edge for the column of numbers and an even left-hand edge for
    B. right-hand edge for both the column of numbers and
    C. left-hand edge for the column of numbers and an even right-hand edge for
    D. left-hand edge for both the column of numbers and

18.____

3 (#1)

83

19. The word *re*, when used in a memorandum, refers to the information that is on the _____ line. 19._____
    A. identification   B. subject   C. attention   D. reference

20. Of the following uses of the period, the one which requires NO spacing after it when it is typed is when the period 20._____
    A. follows an abbreviation or an initial
    B. follows a figure or letter at the beginning of a line in a list of items
    C. comes between the initials that make up a single abbreviation
    D. comes at the end of a sentence

21. This <u>mark</u> is a proofreader's mark meaning the word 21._____
    A. is misspelled
    B. should be underlined
    C. should be bold
    D. should be capitalized

22. When typing a report that is double-spaced, the STANDARD recommended practice for indicating the start of new paragraphs is to 22._____
    A. double-space between paragraphs and indent the first word at least five spaces
    B. triple-space between paragraphs and indent the first word at least five spaces
    C. triple-space between paragraphs and type block style at the margin
    D. double-space between paragraphs and type block style at the margin

23. In order to center a heading on a sheet of paper once the center of the paper has been found, the EASIEST and MOST efficient method to use is 23._____
    A. note the scale at each end of the heading to be centered and divide by two
    B. backspace from the center of the paper one space for every two letters and spaces in the heading
    C. arrange the heading around the middle number on the computer
    D. use a ruler to mark off the amount of space from both sides of the center of the paper that should be taken up by the heading

24. You are about to type a single-spaced letter from a typewritten draft. In order to center this letter from top to bottom, your FIRST step should be to 24._____
    A. determine the number of spaces needed for the top and bottom margins
    B. determine the number of spaces needed for the left and right margins
    C. count the number of lines, including blank ones, which will be used for the letter
    D. subtract from the number of writing lines on the sheet of paper the number of lines that will not be used for the letter

25. When typing a table which lists several amounts of money and the total in a column, the dollar sign should be placed in front of the 25._____
    A. first dollar amount only
    B. total dollar amount only
    C. first and total dollar amounts only
    D. all of the amounts of money in the column

26. If a legal document is being prepared and requires necessary information to be typed into blank areas on preprinted legal forms, the margins for a line of typewritten material should be determined PRIMARILY by
    A. counting the total number of words to be typed
    B. the margins set for the pre-printed matter
    C. spacing backwards from the right margin rule
    D. the estimated width and height of the material to be entered

26.____

27. When checking for errors in material you've typed, it is BEST to
    A. proofread the material and use the spell-check function in combination
    B. give the material to someone else to review
    C. run the spell-check function and auto-correct all found errors
    D. proofread the material then e-mail it to another typist for final approval

27.____

28. Assume that Mr. Frank Foran is an acting official. In a letter written to him, the word *acting* would
    A. be used with the title in the address and in the salutation
    B. not be used with the title in the address
    C. be used with the title in the address but not in the salutation
    D. not be used with the title in the address or in the salutation

28.____

29. The software program that requires proficiency in typing in order to best utilize its MOST important features is
    A. Microsoft Excel   B. Adobe Reader
    C. Microsoft Word   D. Intuit QuickBooks

29.____

30. The MAIN reason for keeping a careful record of incoming mail is that
    A. greater speed and accuracy is obtained for answering outgoing mail
    B. this record is legal evidence
    C. it develops the efficiency of the office clerks
    D. the information may be useful some day

30.____

KEY (CORRECT ANSWERS)

1.	C	11.	C	21.	D
2.	D	12.	D	22.	A
3.	B	13.	D	23.	B
4.	B	14.	B	24.	C
5.	C	15.	D	25.	C
6.	A	16.	B	26.	B
7.	D	17.	C	27.	A
8.	C	18.	A	28.	C
9.	B	19.	B	29.	C
10.	A	20.	C	30.	A

TEST 2

DIRECTIONS: Each question or incomplete statement is followed by several suggested answers or completions. Select the one that BEST answers the question or completes the statement. *PRINT THE LETTER OF THE CORRECT ANSWER IN THE SPACE AT THE RIGHT.*

Questions 1-4.

DIRECTIONS: Questions 1 through 4 are to be answered SOLELY on the basis of the information contained in the following passage which is taken from a typing test.

    Modern office methods, geared to ever higher speeds and aimed at ever greater efficiency, are largely the result of the typewriter. The typewriter is a substitute for handwriting; and, in the hands of a skilled typist, not only turns out letters and other documents at least three times faster than a penman can do the work, but turns out the greater volume more uniformly and legibly. With the use of carbon paper and onionskin paper, identical copies can be made at the same time.

    The typewriter, besides its effect on the conduct of business and government, has had a very important effect on the position of women. The typewriter has done much to bring women into business and government, and today there are vastly more women than men typists. Many women have used the keys of the typewriter to climb the ladder to responsible managerial positions.

    The typewriter, as its name implies, employs type to make an ink impression on paper. For many years, the manual typewriter was the standard machine used. Today, the electric typewriter is dominant, with electronic typewriters, word processors, and computers coming into wider use.

    The mechanism of the office manual typewriter includes a set of keys arranged systematically in rows; a semicircular frame of type, connected to the keys by levers; the carriage or paper carrier; a rubber roller called a platen, against which the type strikes; and an inked ribbon which makes the impression of the type character when the key strikes it. This machine, once omnipresent, is an antique today.

1. The above passage mentions a number of good features of the combination of a skilled typist and a typewriter.
   Of the following, the feature which is NOT mentioned in the passage is
     A. speed   B. uniformity   C. reliability   D. legibility

   1.____

2. According to the above passage, a skilled typist can
     A. turn out at least five carbon copies of typed matter
     B. type at least three times faster than a penman can write
     C. type more than 80 words a minute
     D. readily move into a managerial position

   2.____

3. According to the above passage, which of the following is NOT part of the mechanism of a manual typewriter?
   A. Carbon paper
   B. Paper carrier
   C. Platen
   D. Inked ribbon

4. According to the above passage, the typewriter has helped
   A. men more than women in business
   B. women in career advancement into management
   C. men and women equally, but women have taken better advantage of it
   D. more women than men, because men generally dislike routine typing work

5. Standard rules for typing spacing have developed through usage. According to these rules, two spaces are left after a(n)
   A. colon
   B. comma
   C. hyphen
   D. opening parenthesis

6. Assume that you have to type the heading CENTERING TYPED HEADINGS on a piece of paper which extends from 0 to 100 on the typewriter scale. You want the heading to be perfectly centered on the paper.
   In order to find the proper point on the typewriter scale at which to begin typing, you should determine the paper's center point on the typewriter scale and then _____ the number of letters and spaces in the heading.
   A. add
   B. add one-half
   C. subtract
   D. subtract one-half

7. While typing from a rough draft, the practice of reading a line ahead of what you are now typing is considered to be a
   A. *good* practice; it may prepare your fingers for the words which you will be typing
   B. *good* practice; it may help you to review the subject matter contained in the material
   C. *poor* practice; it may increase your typing speed so that your accuracy is decreased
   D. *poor* practice; it may cause you to lose your concentration and make errors in the words you are presently typing

8. Assume that you are transcribing a letter and you are not sure how to divide a word at the end of a line you are typing.
   The BEST way to determine where to divide the word is by
   A. asking your supervisor
   B. asking the person who dictated the letter
   C. checking with other stenographers
   D. looking up the word in a dictionary

9. When taking proper care of a typewriter, it is NOT a desirable action to
    A. clean the feed rolls with a cloth
    B. dust the exterior surface of the machine
    C. oil the rubber parts of the machine
    D. use a type-cleaning brush to clean the keys

10. Of the following, the LEAST desirable action to take when typing a rough draft of a report is to
    A. cross out typing errors instead of erasing them
    B. double or triple space between lines
    C. provide large margins on all sides of the typing paper
    D. use letterhead or onionskin paper

11. The date line of every business letter should indicate the month, the day of the month, and the year.
    The MOST common practice when typing a date line is to type it as
    A. Jan. 12, 2018   B. January 12, 2018
    C. 1-12-18   D. 1/12/18

Questions 12-16.

DIRECTIONS: Questions 12 through 16 are to be answered SOLELY on the basis of the information provided in the following passage.

A written report is a communication of information from one person to another. It is an account of some matter especially investigated, however routine that matter may be. The ultimate basis of any good written report is facts, which became known through observation and verification. Good written reports may seem to be no more than general ideas and opinions. However, in such cases, the facts leading to these opinions were gathered, verified, and reported earlier, and the opinions are dependent upon these facts. Good style, proper form, and emphasis cannot make a good written report out of unreliable information and bad judgments but on the other hand, solid investigation and brilliant thinking are not likely to become very useful until they are effectively communicated to others. If a person's work calls for written reports, then his work is often no better than his written reports.

12. Based on the information in the above passage, it can be concluded that opinions expressed in a report should be
    A. based on facts which are gathered and reported
    B. emphasized repeatedly when they result from a special investigation
    C. kept to a minimum
    D. separated from the body of the report

13. In the above passage, the one of the following which is mentioned as a way of establishing facts is
    A. authority   B. communication
    C. reporting   D. verification

14. According to the above passage, the characteristic shared by ALL written reports is that they are
    A. accounts of routine matters
    B. transmissions of information
    C. reliable and logical
    D. written in proper form

15. Which of the following conclusions can LOGICALLY be drawn from the information given in the above passage?
    A. Brilliant thinking can make up for unreliable information in a report.
    B. One method of judging an individual's work is the quality of the written reports he is required to submit.
    C. Proper form and emphasis can make a good report out of unreliable information.
    D. Good written reports that seem to be no more than general ideas should be rewritten.

16. Which of the following suggested titles would be MOST appropriate for this passage?
    A. GATHERING AND ORGANIZING FACTS
    B. TECHNIQUES OF OBSERVATION
    C. NATURE AND PURPOSE OF REPORTS
    D. REPORTS AND OPINIONS: DIFFERENCES AND SIMILARITIES

Questions 17-25

DIRECTIONS: Each of Questions 17 through 25 consists of a sentence which may or may not be an example of good English usage. Examine each sentence, considering grammar, punctuation, spelling, capitalization, and awkwardness. Then choose the correct statement about it from the four choices below it. If the English usage in the sentence given is better than any of the changes suggested in Choices B, C, or D, pick choice A. Do NOT pick a choice that will change the meaning of the sentence.

17. We attended a staff conference on Wednesday the new safety and fire rules were discussed.
    A. This is an example of acceptable writing.
    B. The words *safety*, *fire*, and *rules* should begin with capital letters.
    C. There should be a comma after the word *Wednesday*.
    D. There should be a period after the word *Wednesday*, and the word *the* should begin with a capital letter.

18. Neither the dictionary or the telephone directory could be found in the office library.
    A. This is an example of acceptable writing.
    B. The word *or* should be changed to *nor*.
    C. The word *library* should be spelled *libery*.
    D. The word *neither* should be changed to *either*.

19. The report would have been typed correctly if the typist cold read the draft. 19.____
    A. This is an example of acceptable writing.
    B. The word *would* should be removed.
    C. The word *have* should be inserted after the word *could*.
    D. The word *correctly* should be changed to *correct*.

20. The supervisor brought the reports and forms to an employees desk. 20.____
    A. This is an example of acceptable writing.
    B. The word *brought* should be changed to *took*.
    C. There should be a comma after the word *reports* and a comma after the word *forms*.
    D. The word *employees* should be spelled *employee's*.

21. It's important for all the office personnel to submit their vacation schedules on time. 21.____
    A. This is an example of acceptable writing.
    B. The word *It's* should be spelled *Its*.
    C. The word *their* should be spelled *they're*.
    D. The word *personnel* should be spelled *personal*.

22. The supervisor wants that all staff members report to the office at 9:00 A.M. 22.____
    A. This is an example of acceptable writing.
    B. The word *that* should be removed and the word *to* should be inserted after the word *members*.
    C. There should be a comma after the word *wants* and a comma after the word *office*.
    D. The word *wants* should be changed to *want* and the word *shall* should be inserted after the word *members*.

23. Every morning the clerk opens the office mail and distributes it. 23.____
    A. This is an example of acceptable writing.
    B. The word *opens* should be changed to *open*.
    C. The word *mail* should be changed to *letters*.
    D. The word *it* should be changed to *them*.

24. The secretary typed more fast on an electric typewriter than on a manual typewriter. 24.____
    A. This is an example of acceptable writing.
    B. The words *more fast* should be changed to *faster*.
    C. There should be a comma after the words *electric typewriter*.
    D. The word *than* should be changed to *then*.

25. The new stenographer needed a desk a typewriter, a chair and a blotter. 25.____
    A. This is an example of acceptable writing.
    B. The word *blotter* should be spelled *blodder*.
    C. The word *stenographer* should begin with a capital letter.
    D. There should be a comma after the word *desk*.

KEY (CORRECT ANSWERS)

1.	C	11.	B
2.	B	12	A
3.	A	13.	D
4.	B	14.	B
5.	A	15.	B
6.	D	16.	C
7.	D	17.	D
8.	D	18.	B
9.	C	19.	C
10.	D	20.	D

21. A
22. B
23. A
24. B
25. D

EXAMINATION SECTION
TEST 1

DIRECTIONS: Each question or incomplete statement is followed by several suggested answers or completions. Select the one that BEST answers the question or completes the statement. *PRINT THE LETTER OF THE CORRECT ANSWER IN THE SPACE AT THE RIGHT.*

Questions 1-22.

DIRECTIONS: Read through each group of words. Indicate in the space at the right the letter of the misspelled word.

1. A. miniature   B. recession   1.____
    C. accommodate D. supress

2. A. mortgage   B. illogical   2.____
    C. fasinate   D. pronounce

3. A. calendar   B. heros   3.____
    C. ecstasy   D. librarian

4. A. initiative   B. extraordinary 4.____
    C. villian   D. exaggerate

5. A. absence   B. sense   5.____
    C. dosn't   D. height

6. A. curiosity   B. ninety   6.____
    C. truely   D. grammar

7. A. amateur   B. definate   7.____
    C. meant   D. changeable

8. A. excellent   B. studioes   8.____
    C. achievement D. weird

9. A. goverment   B. description 9.____
    C. sergeant   D. desirable

10. A. proceed   B. anxious   10.____
    C. neice   D. precede

11. A. environment B. omitted   11.____
    C. apparant   D. misconstrue

12. A. comparative B. hindrance   12.____
    C. benefited   D. unamimous

13. A. embarrass B. recommend
    C. desciple D. argument

14. A. sophomore B. suprintendent
    C. concievable D. disastrous

15. A. agressive B. questionnaire
    C. occurred D. rhythm

16. A. peaceable B. conscientious
    C. redicule D. deterrent

17. A. mischievious B. writing
    C. competition D. athletics

18. A. auxiliary B. synonymous
    C. maneuver D. repitition

19. A. existence B. optimistic
    C. acquitted D. tragedy

20. A. hypocrisy B. parrallel
    C. exhilaration D. prevalent

21. A. convalesence B. infallible
    C. destitute D. grotesque

22. A. magnanimity B. asassination
    C. incorrigible D. pestilence

Questions 23-40.

DIRECTIONS: In Questions 23 through 40, one sentence fragment contains an error in punctuation or capitalization. Indicate the letter of the INCORRECT sentence fragment and place it in the space at the right.

23. A. Despite a year's work
    B. in a well-equipped laboratory
    C. my Uncle failed to complete his research
    D. now he will never graduate.

24. A. Gene, if you are going to sleep
    B. all afternoon I will enter
    C. that ladies' golf tournament
    D. sponsored by the Chamber of Commerce.

3 (#1)

25. A. Seeing the cat slink toward the barn,
    B. the farmer's wife jumped off the
    C. ladder picked up a broom, and began
    D. shouting at the top of her voice.

    25.____

26. A. Extending over southeast Idaho and
    B. northwest Wyoming, the Tetons
    C. are noted for their height; however the
    D. highest peak is actually under 14,000 feet.

    26.____

27. A. "Sarah, can you recall the name
    B. of the English queen
    C. who supposedly said, 'We are not
    D. amused?"

    27.____

28. A. My aunt's graduation present to me
    B. cost, I imagine more than she could
    C. actually afford. It's a
    D. Swiss watch with numerous features.

    28.____

29. A. On the left are examples of buildings
    B. from the Classical Period; two temples
    C. one of which was dedicated to Zeus; the
    D. Agora, a marketplace; and a large arch.

    29.____

30. A. Tired of sonic booms, the people who
    B. live near Springfield's Municipal Airport
    C. formed an anti noise organization
    D. with the amusing name of Sound Off.

    30.____

31. A. "Joe, Mrs. Sweeney said, "your family
    B. arrives Sunday. Since you'll be in
    C. the Labor Day parade, we could ask Mr.
    D. Krohn, who has a big car, to meet them."

    31.____

32. A. The plumber emerged from the basement and
    B. said, "Mr. Cohen I found the trouble in
    C. your water heater. Could you move those
    D. Schwinn bikes out of my way?"

    32.____

33. A. The President walked slowly to the
    B. podium, bowed to Edward Everett Hale
    C. the other speaker, and began his formal address:
    D. "Fourscore and seven years ago...."

    33.____

34. A. Mr. Fontana, I hope, will arrive before
    B. the beginning of the ceremonies; however,
    C. if his plane is delayed, I have a substitute
    D. speaker who can be here at a moments' notice.

    34.____

35.
A. Gladys wedding dress, a satin creation,
B. lay crumpled on the floor; her veil,
C. torn and streaked, lay nearby. "Jilted!"
D. shrieked Gladys. She was clearly annoyed.

36.
A. Although it is poor grammar, the word
B. hopefully has become television's newest
C. pet expression; I hope (to use the correct
D. form) that it will soon pass from favor.

37.
A.   Plaza Apartment Hotel
B.   103 Tower road
C.   Hampstead, Iowa 52025
D.   March 13, 2021

38.
A. Circulation Department
B. British History Illustrated
C. 3000 Walnut Street
D. Boulder Colorado 80302

39.
A. Dear Sirs:
B. Last spring I ordered a subscription to your
C. magazine. I had read and enjoyed the May
D. issue containing the article titled "kings."

40.
A. I have not however, received a
B. single issue. Will you check this?
C. Sincerely,
D. Maria Herrera

Questions 41-70.

DIRECTIONS: Questions 41 through 70 represent common grammatical concerns: subject-verb agreement, appropriate use of pronouns, and appropriate use of verbs. Read each sentence and indicate the letter of the grammatically CORRECT answer in the space at the right.

41. THE REIVERS, one of William Faulkner's last works, _____ made into a movie starring Steve McQueen.
   A. has been   B. have been   C. are being   D. were

42. He _____ on the ground, his eyes fastened on an ant slowly pushing a morsel of food toward the ant hill.
   A. layed   B. laid   C. had laid   D. lay

43. Nobody in the tri-cities _____ to admit that a flood could be disastrous.
   A. are willing   B. have been willing
   C. is willing   D. were willing

44. "_____," the senator asked, "have you convinced to run against the incumbent?"
    A. Who   B. Whom   C. Whomever   D. Womsoever

45. Of all the psychology courses that I took, Statistics 101 _____ the most demanding.
    A. was   B. are   C. is   D. were

46. Neither the conductor nor the orchestra members _____ the music to be applauded so enthusiastically.
    A. were expecting
    B. was expecting
    C. is expected
    D. has been expecting

47. The requirements for admission to the Lettermen's Club _____ posted outside the athletic director's office for months.
    A. was   B. was being   C. has been   D. have been

48. Please give me a list of the people _____ to compete in the kayak race.
    A. whom you think have planned
    B. who you think has planned
    C. who you think is planning
    D. who you think are planning

49. I saw Eloise and Abelard earlier today; _____ were riding around in a fancy 1956 MG.
    A. she and him   B. her and him   C. she and he   D. her and he

50. If you _____ the trunk in the attic, I'll unpack it later today.
    A. can sit
    B. are able to sit
    C. can set
    D. have sat

51. _____ all of the flour been used, or may I borrow three cups?
    A. Have   B. Has   C. Is   D. Could

52. In exasperation, the cycle shop's owner suggested that _____ there too long.
    A. us boys were
    B. we boys were
    C. us boys had been
    D. we boys had been

53. Idleness as well as money _____ the root of all evil.
    A. have been
    B. were to have been
    C. is
    D. are

54. Only the string players from the quartet—Gregory, Isaac, ____—remained after the concert to answer questions.
    A. him, and I
    B. he, and I
    C. him, and me
    D. he, and me

55. Of all the antiques that _____ for sale, Gertrude chose to buy a stupid glass thimble.
    A. was
    B. is
    C. would have
    D. were

56. The detective snapped, "Don't confuse me with theories about _____ you believe committed the crime!"
    A. who B. whom C. whomever D. which

57. _____ when we first called, we might have avoided our present predicament.
    A. The plumber's coming
    B. If the plumber would have come
    C. If the plumber had come
    D. If the plumber was to have come

58. We thought the sun _____ in the north until we discovered that our compass was defective.
    A. had rose
    B. had risen
    C. had rised
    D. had raised

59. Each play of Shakespeare's _____ more than _____ share of memorable characters.
    A. contain its
    B. contains; its
    C. contains; it's
    D. contain; their

60. Our English teacher suggested to _____ seniors that either Tolstoy or Dickens _____ the outstanding novelist of the nineteenth century.
    A. we; was considered
    B. we; were considered
    C. us; was considered
    D. us; were considered

61. Sherlock Holmes, together with his great friend and companion Dr. Watson, _____ to aid the woman _____ had stumbled into the room.
    A. has agreed; who
    B. have agreed; whom
    C. has agreed; whom
    D. have agreed; who

62. Several of the deer _____ when they spotted my backpack _____ open in the meadow.
    A. was frightened; laying
    B. were frightened; lying
    C. were frightened; laying
    D. was frightened; lying

63. After the Scholarship Committee announces _____ selection, hysterics often _____.
    A. it's; occur
    B. its; occur
    C. their; occur
    D. their; occurs

64. I _____ the key on the table last night so you and _____ could find it.
    A. layed; her
    B. lay; she
    C. laid; she
    D. laid; her

65. Some of the antelope _____ wandered away from the meadow where the rancher _____ the block of salt.
    A. has; sat
    B. has; set
    C. have; had set
    D. has; sets

66. Macaroni and cheese _____ best to us (that is, to Andy and _____) when Mother adds extra cheddar cheese.
    A. tastes; I
    B. tastes; me
    C. taste; me
    D. taste; I

66.____

67. Frank said, "It must have been _____ called the phone company."
    A. she who
    B. she whom
    C. her who
    D. her whom

67.____

68. The herd _____ moving restlessly at every bolt of lightning; it was either Ted or _____ who saw the beginning of the stampede.
    A. was; me
    B. were; I
    C. was; I
    D. have been; me

68.____

69. The foreman _____ his lateness by saying that his alarm clock _____ until six minutes before eight.
    A. explains; had not rang
    B. explained; has not rung
    C. has explained; rung
    D. explained; hadn't rung

69.____

70. Of all the coaches, Ms. Cox is the only one who _____ that Sherry dives more gracefully than _____.
    A. is always saying; I
    B. is always saying; me
    C. are always saying; I
    D. were always saying; me

70.____

Questions 71-90.

DIRECTIONS: Choose the word in Questions 71 through 90 that is MOST opposite in meaning to the italicized word.

71. *fact*
    A. statistic
    B. statement
    C. incredible
    D. conjecture

71.____

72. *stiff*
    A. fastidious
    B. babble
    C. supple
    D. apprehensive

72.____

73. *blunt*
    A. concise
    B. tactful
    C. artistic
    D. humble

73.____

74. *foreign*
    A. pertinent
    B. comely
    C. strange
    D. scrupulous

74.____

75. *anger*
    A. infer
    B. pacify
    C. taint
    D. revile

75.____

76. *frank*
    A. earnest
    B. reticent
    C. post
    D. expensive

76.____

8 (#1)

77. *secure*
    A. precarious B. acquire C. moderate D. frenzied

78. *petty*
    A. harmonious B. careful
    C. forthright D. momentous

79. *concede*
    A. dispute B. reciprocate
    C. subvert D. propagate

80. *benefit*
    A. liquidation B. bazaar
    C. detriment D. profit

81. *capricious*
    A. preposterous B. constant
    C. diabolical D. careless

82. *boisterous*
    A. devious B. valiant C. girlish D. taciturn

83. *harmony*
    A. congruence B. discord C. chagrin D. melody

84. *laudable*
    A. auspicious B. despicable
    C. acclaimed D. doubtful

85. *adherent*
    A. partisan B. stoic C. renegade D. recluse

86. *exuberant*
    A. frail B. corpulent C. austere D. bigot

87. *spurn*
    A. accede B. flail C. efface D. annihilate

88. *spontaneous*
    A. hapless B. corrosive
    C. intentional D. willful

89. *disparage*
    A. abolish B. exude C. incriminate D. extol

90. *timorous*
    A. succinct B. chaste C. audacious D. insouciant

KEY (CORRECT ANSWERS)

1. D	21. A	41. A	61. A	81. B
2. C	22. B	42. D	62.	82. D
3. B	23. C	43. C	63. B	83. B
4. C	24. B	44. B	64. C	84. B
5. C	25. C	45. A	65. C	85. C
6. C	26. C	46. A	66. B	86. C
7. B	27. D	47. D	67. A	87. A
8. B	28. B	48. A	68. C	88. C
9. A	29. B	49. C	69. D	89. D
10. C	30. C	50. C	70. A	90. C
11. C	31. A	51. B	71. D	
12. D	32. B	52. D	72. C	
13. C	33. B	53. C	73. B	
14. C	34. D	54. B	74. A	
15. A	35. A	55. D	75. B	
16. C	36. B	56. B	76. B	
17. A	37. B	57. C	77. A	
18. D	38. D	58. B	78. D	
19. B	39. D	59. B	79. A	
20. B	40. A	60. C	80. C	

SPELLING

EXAMINATION SECTION

TEST 1

DIRECTIONS: Each question or incomplete statement is followed by several suggested answers or completions. Select the one that BEST answers the question or completes the statement. *PRINT THE LETTER OF THE CORRECT ANSWER IN THE SPACE AT THE RIGHT.*

Questions 1-5.

DIRECTIONS: Questions 1 through 5 consist of four words. Indicate the letter of the word that is CORRECTLY spelled.

1. A. harassment   B. harrasment   1.____
    C. harasment   D. harrassment

2. A. maintainance   B. maintenence   2.____
    C. maintainence   D. maintenance

3. A. comparable   B. comprable   3.____
    C. comparible   D. commparable

4. A. suficient   B. sufficiant   4.____
    C. sufficient   D. suficiant

5. A. fairly   B. fairley   C. farely   D. fairlie   5.____

Questions 6-10.

DIRECTIONS: Questions 6 through 10 consist of four words. Indicate the letter of the word that is INCORRECTLY spelled.

6. A. pallor   B. ballid   C. ballet   D. pallid   6.____

7. A. urbane   B. surburbane   7.____
    C. interurban   D. urban

8. A. facial   B. physical   C. fiscle   D. muscle   8.____

9. A. interceed   B. benefited   9.____
    C. analogous   D. altogether

10. A. seizure   B. irrelevant   10.____
    C. inordinate   D. dissapproved

103

KEY (CORRECT ANSWERS)

1.	A	6.	B
2.	D	7.	B
3.	A	8.	C
4.	C	9.	A
5.	A	10.	D

TEST 2

DIRECTIONS: Each of Questions 1 through 15 consists of two words preceded by the letters A and B. In each question, one of the words may be spelled INCORRECTLY or both words may be spelled CORRECTLY. If one of the words in a question is spelled INCORRECTLY, print in the space at the right the capital letter preceding the INCORRECTLY spelled word. If both words are spelled CORRECTLY, print the letter C.

1. A. easely   B. readily   1.____
2. A. pursue   B. decend   2.____
3. A. measure   B. laboratory   3.____
4. A. exausted   B. traffic   4.____
5. A. discussion   B. unpleasant   5.____
6. A. campaign   B. murmer   6.____
7. A. guarantee   B. sanatary   7.____
8. A. communication B. safty   8.____
9. A. numerus   B. celebration   9.____
10. A. nourish   B. begining   10.____
11. A. courious   B. witness   11.____
12. A. undoubtedly   B. thoroughly   12.____
13. A. accessible   B. artifical   13.____
14. A. feild   B. arranged   14.____
15. A. admittence   B. hastily   15.____

KEY (CORRECT ANSWERS)

1. A	6. B	11. A
2. B	7. B	12. C
3. C	8. B	13. B
4. A	9. A	14. A
5. C	10. B	15. A

TEST 3

DIRECTIONS: In each of the following sentences, one word is misspelled. Following each sentence is a list of four words taken from the sentence. Indicate the letter of the word which is MISSPELLED in the sentence. *PRINT THE LETTER OF THE CORRECT ANSWER IN THE SPACE AT THE RIGHT.*

1. The placing of any inflammable substance in any building, or the placing of any device or contrivance capable of producing fire, for the purpose of causing a fire is an attempt to burn.
    A. inflammable
    B. substance
    C. device
    D. contrivence

    1.____

2. The word *break* also means obtaining an entrance into a building by any artifice used for that purpose, or by collussion with any person therein.
    A. obtaining
    B. entrance
    C. artifice
    D. colussion

    2.____

3. Any person who with intent to provoke a breech of the peace causes a disturbance or is offensive to others may be deemed to have committed disorderly conduct.
    A. breech
    B. disturbance
    C. offensive
    D. committed

    3.____

4. When the offender inflicts a grevious harm upon the person from whose possession, or in whose presence, property is taken, he is guilty of robbery.
    A. offender
    B. grevious
    C. possession
    D. presence

    4.____

5. A person who wilfuly encourages or advises another person in attempting to take the latter's life is guilty of a felony.
    A. wilfuly
    B. encourages
    C. advises
    D. attempting

    5.____

6. He maliciously demurred to an ajournment of the proceedings.
    A. maliciously
    B. demurred
    C. ajournment
    D. proceedings

    6.____

7. His innocence at that time is irrelevant in view of his more recent villianous demeanor.
    A. innocence
    B. irrelevant
    C. villianous
    D. demeanor

    7.____

8. The mischievous boys aggrevated the annoyance of their neighbor.
    A. mischievous
    B. aggrevated
    C. annoyance
    D. neighbor

    8.____

2 (#3)

9. While his perseverence was commendable, his judgment was debatable. 9.____
   A. perseverence B. commendable
   C. judgment D. debatable

10. He was hoping the appeal would facilitate his aquittal. 10.____
    A. hoping B. appeal
    C. facilitate D. aquittal

11. It would be preferable for them to persue separate courses. 11.____
    A. preferable B. persue
    C. separate D. courses

12. The litigant was complimented on his persistance and achievement. 12.____
    A. litigant B. complimented
    C. persistance D. achievement

13. Ocassionally there are discrepancies in the descriptions of miscellaneous items. 13.____
    A. ocassionally B. discrepancies
    C. descriptions D. miscellaneous

14. The councilmanic seargent-at-arms enforced the prohibition. 14.____
    A. councilmanic B. seargeant-at-arms
    C. enforced D. prohibition

15. The teacher had an ingenious device for maintaining attendance. 15.____
    A. ingenious B. device
    C. maintaning D. attendance

16. A worrysome situation has developed as a result of the assessment that absenteeism is increasing despite our conscientious efforts. 16.____
    A. worrysome B. assessment
    C. absenteeism D. conscientious

17. I concurred with the credit manager that it was practicable to charge purchases on a biennial basis, and the company agreed to adhear to this policy. 17.____
    A. concurred B. practicable
    C. biennial D. adhear

18. The pastor was chagrined and embarassed by the irreverent conduct of one of his parishioners. 18.____
    A. chagrined B. embarassed
    C. irreverent D. parishioners

19. His inate seriousness was belied by his flippant demeanor. 19.____
    A. inate B. belied
    C. flippant D. demeanor

20. It was exceedingly regrettable that the excessive number of challenges in the court delayed the start of the trial. 20.____
    A. exceedingly
    B. regrettable
    C. excessive
    D. challanges

KEY (CORRECT ANSWERS)

1.	D	11.	B
2.	D	12.	C
3.	A	13.	A
4.	B	14.	B
5.	A	15.	C
6.	C	16.	A
7.	C	17.	D
8.	B	18.	B
9.	A	19.	A
10.	D	20.	D

TEST 4

Questions 1-11.

DIRECTIONS: Each question consists of three words in each question, one of the words may be spelled incorrectly or all three may be spelled correctly. For each question if one of the words is spelled INCORRECTLY, write the letter of the incorrect word in the space at the right. If all three words are spelled CORRECTLY, write the letter D in the space at the right.

SAMPLE I: (A) guide   (B) departmint   (C) stranger
SAMPLE II: (A) comply   (B) valuable   (C) window

In Sample I, departmint is incorrect. It should be spelled department. Therefore, B is the answer.
In Sample II, all three words are spelled correctly. Therefore, D is the answer.

1. A. argument   B. reciept   C. complain   1.____
2. A. sufficient   B. postpone   C. visible   2.____
3. A. expirience   B. dissatisly   C. alternate   3.____
4. A. occurred   B. noticable   C. appendix   4.____
5. A. anxious   B. guarantee   C. calendar   5.____
6. A. sincerely   B. affectionately C. truly   6.____
7. A. excellant   B. verify   C. important   7.____
8. A. error   B. quality   C. enviroment   8.____
9. A. exercise   B. advance   C. pressure   9.____
10. A. citizen   B. expence   C. memory   10.____
11. A. flexable   B. focus   C. forward   11.____

Questions 12-15.

DIRECTIONS: Each of Questions 12 through 15 consists of a group of four words. Examine each group carefully; then in the space at the right, indicate
A. if only one word in the group is spelled correctly
B. if two words in the group are spelled correctly
C. if three words in the group are spelled correctly
D. if all four words in the group are spelled correctly

12. Wendsday, particular, similar, hunderd   12.____

13. realize, judgment, opportunities, consistent   13.____

14. equel, principle, assistense, committee   14.____

15. simultaneous, privilege, advise, ocassionaly   15.____

KEY (CORRECT ANSWERS)

1.	B	6.	D	11.	A
2.	D	7.	A	12.	B
3.	A	8.	C	13.	D
4.	B	9.	D	14.	A
5.	C	10.	B	15.	C

TEST 5

DIRECTIONS: Each of Questions 1 through 15 consists of two words preceded by the letters A and B. In each item, one of the words may be spelled INCORRECTLY or both words may be spelled CORRECTLY. If one of the words in a question is spelled INCORRECTLY, print in the space at the right the letter preceding the INCORRECTLY spelled word. If bot words are spelled CORRECTLY, print the letter C.

1. A. justified   B. offering   1.____
2. A. predjudice   B. license   2.____
3. A. label   B. pamphlet   3.____
4. A. bulletin   B. physical   4.____
5. A. assure   B. exceed   5.____
6. A. advantagous   B. evident   6.____
7. A. benefit   B. occured   7.____
8. A. acquire   B. graditude   8.____
9. A. amenable   B. boundry   9.____
10. A. deceive   B. voluntary   10.____
11. A. imunity   B. conciliate   11.____
12. A. acknoledge   B. presume   12.____
13. A. substitute   B. prespiration   13.____
14. A. reputable   B. announce   14.____
15. A. luncheon   B. wretched   15.____

KEY (CORRECT ANSWERS)

1.	C	6.	A	11.	A
2.	A	7.	B	12.	A
3.	C	8.	B	13.	B
4.	C	9.	B	14.	A
5.	C	10.	C	15.	C

TEST 6

DIRECTIONS: Questions 1 through 15 contain lists of words, one of which is misspelled. Indicate the MISSPELLED word in each group. *PRINT THE LETTER OF THE CORRECT ANSWER IN THE SPACE AT THE RIGHT.*

1. A. felony B. lacerate 1.____
   C. cancellation D. seperate

2. A. batallion B. beneficial 2.____
   C. miscellaneous D. secretary

3. A. camouflage B. changeable 3.____
   C. embarrass D. inoculate

4. A. beneficial B. disasterous 4.____
   C. incredible D. miniature

5. A. auxilliary B. hypocrisy 5.____
   C. phlegm D. vengeance

6. A. aisle B. cemetary 6.____
   C. courtesy D. extraordinary

7. A. crystallize B. innoculate 7.____
   C. eminent D. symmetrical

8. A. judgment B. maintainance 8.____
   C. bouillon D. eery

9. A. isosceles B. ukulele 9.____
   C. mayonaise D. iridescent

10. A. remembrance B. occurence 10.____
    C. correspondence D. countenance

11. A. corpuscles B. mischievous 11.____
    C. batchelor D. bulletin

12. A. terrace B. banister 12.____
    C. concrete D. masonery

13. A. balluster B. gutter 13.____
    C. latch D. bridging

14. A. personnell B. navel 14.____
    C. therefor D. emigrant

112

15. A. committee   B. submiting   15._____
     C. amendment   D. electorate

KEY (CORRECT ANSWERS)

1.	D	6.	B	11.	C
2.	A	7.	B	12.	D
3.	C	8.	B	13.	A
4.	B	9.	C	14.	A
5.	A	10.	B	15.	B

TEST 7

Questions 1-5.

DIRECTIONS: Questions 1 through 5 consist of groups of four words. Select answer
A if only one word is spelled correctly in a group
B if TWO words are spelled correctly in a group
C if THREE words are spelled correctly in a group
D if all FOUR words are spelled correctly in a group.

1. counterfeit, embarass, panicky, supercede   1.____

2. benefited, personnel, questionnaire, unparalelled   2.____

3. bankruptcy, describable, proceed, vacuum   3.____

4. handicapped, mispell, offerred, pilgrimmage   4.____

5. corduroy, interfere, privilege, separator   5.____

Questions 6-10.

DIRECTIONS: Questions 6 through 10 consist of four pairs of words each. Some of the words are spelled correctly; others are spelled incorrectly. For each question, indicate in the space at the right the letter preceding that pair of words in which BOTH words are spelled CORRECTLY.

6. A. hygienic, inviegle   B. omniscience, pittance   6.____
   C. plagarize, nullify   D. seargent, perilous

7. A. auxilary, existence   B. pronounciation, accordance   7.____
   C. ignominy, indegence   D. suable, baccalaureate

8. A. discreet, inaudible   B. hypocrisy, currupt   8.____
   C. liquidate, maintainance   D. transparancy, onerous

9. A. facility; stimulent   B. frugel, sanitary   9.____
   C. monetary, prefatory   D. punctileous, credentials

10. A. bankruptsy, perceptible   B. disuade, resilient   10.____
    C. exhilerate, expectancy   D. panegyric, disparate

Questions 11-15.

DIRECTIONS: Each question or incomplete statement is followed by several suggested answers or completions. Select the one that BEST answers the question or completes the statement. PRINT THE LETTER OF THE CORRECT ANSWER IN THE SPACE AT THE RIGHT.

2 (#7)

11. The silent *e* must be retained when the suffix *–able* is added to the word 11.____
    A. argue B. love C. move D. notice

12. The CORRECTLY spelled word in the choices below is 12.____
    A. kindergarden B. zylophone
    C. hemorrhage D. mayonaise

13. Of the following words, the one spelled CORRECTLY is 13.____
    A. begger B. cemetary
    C. embarassed D. coyote

14.
    A. dandilion B. wiry C. sieze D. rythmic 14.____

15. A. beligerent B. anihilation
    C. facetious D. adversery

KEY (CORRECT ANSWERS)

1.	B	6.	B	11.	D
2.	C	7.	D	12.	C
3.	D	8.	A	13.	D
4.	A	9.	C	14.	B
5.	D	10.	D	15.	C

TEST 8

DIRECTIONS: In each of the following sentences, one word is misspelled. Following each sentence is a list of four words taken from the sentence. Indicate the letter of the word which is MISSPELLED. *PRINT THE LETTER OF THE CORRECT ANSWER IN THE SPACE AT THE RIGHT.*

1. If the administrator attempts to withold information, there is a good likelihood that there will be serious repercussions.
    A. administrator
    B. withold
    C. likelihood
    D. repercussions

    1.____

2. He condescended to apologize, but we felt that a beligerent person should not occupy an influential position.
    A. condescended
    B. apologize
    C. beligerent
    D. influential

    2.____

3. Despite the sporadic delinquent payments of his indebtedness, Mr. Johnson has been an exemplery customer.
    A. sporadic
    B. delinquent
    C. indebtedness
    D. exemplery

    3.____

4. He was appreciative of the support he consistantly acquired, but he felt that he had waited an inordinate length of time for it.
    A. appreciative
    B. consistantly
    C. acquired
    D. inordinate

    4.____

5. Undeniably they benefited from the establishment of a receivership, but the question of statutary limitations remained unresolved.
    A. undeniably
    B. benefited
    C. receivership
    D. statutary

    5.____

6. Mr. Smith profered his hand as an indication that he considered it a viable contract, but Mr. Nelson alluded to the fact that his colleagues had not been consulted.
    A. profered
    B. viable
    C. alluded
    D. colleagues

    6.____

7. The treatments were beneficial according to the optomotrists, and the consensus was that minimal improvement could be expected.
    A. beneficial
    B. optomotrists
    C. consensus
    D. minimal

    7.____

8. Her frivolous manner was unbecoming because the air of solemnity at the cemetery was pervasive.
    A. frivalous
    B. solemnity
    C. cemetery
    D. pervasive

    8.____

9. The clandestine meetings were designed to make the two adversaries more amicable, but they served only to intensify their emnity.
    A. clandestine
    B. adversaries
    C. amicable
    D. emnity

10. Do you think that his innovative ideas and financial acumen will help stabalize the fluctuations of the stock market?
    A. innovative
    B. acumen
    C. stabalize
    D. fluctuations

11. In order to keep a perpetual inventory, you will have to keep an uninterrupted surveillance of all the miscellanious stock.
    A. perpetual
    B. uninterrupted
    C. surveillance
    D. miscellanious

12. She used the art of pursuasion on the children because she found that caustic remarks had no perceptible effect on their behavior.
    A. pursuasion
    B. caustic
    C. perceptible
    D. effect

13. His sacreligious outbursts offended his constituents, and he was summarily removed from office by the City Council.
    A. sacreligious
    B. constituents
    C. summarily
    D. Council

14. They exhorted the contestants to greater efforts, but the exhorbitant costs in terms of energy expended resulted in a feeling of lethargy.
    A. exhorted
    B. contestants
    C. exhorbitant
    D. lethargy

15. Since he was knowledgable about illicit drugs, he was served with a subpoena to appear for the prosecution.
    A. knowledgable
    B. illicit
    C. subpoena
    D. prosecution

16. In spite of his lucid statements, they denigrated his report and decided it should be succintly paraphrased.
    A. lucid
    B. denigrated
    C. succintly
    D. paraphrased

17. The discussion was not germane to the contraversy , but the indicted man's insistence on further talk was allowed.
    A. germane
    B. contraversy
    C. indicted
    D. insistence

18. The legislators were enervated by the distances they had traveled during the election year to fullfil their speaking engagements.
    A. legislators
    B. enervated
    C. traveled
    D. fullfil

19. The plaintiffs' attornies charge the defendant in the case with felonious assault. 19.____
    A. plaintiffs'
    B. attornies
    C. defendant
    D. felonious

20. It is symptomatic of the times that we try to placate all, but a proposal for new forms of disciplinery action was promulgated by the staff. 20.____
    A. symptomatic
    B. placate
    C. disciplinery
    D. promulgated

KEY (CORRECT ANSWERS)

1.	B	11.	D
2.	C	12.	A
3.	D	13.	A
4.	B	14.	C
5.	D	15.	A
6.	A	16.	C
7.	B	17.	B
8.	A	18.	D
9.	D	19.	B
10.	C	20.	C

TEST 9

DIRECTIONS: Each of Questions 1 through 15 consists of a single word which is spelled either correctly or incorrectly. If the word is spelled CORRECTLY, you are to print the letter C (Correct) in the space at the right. If the word is spelled INCORRECTL, you are to print the letter W (Wrong).

1. pospone   1._____
2. diffrent   2._____
3. height   3._____
4. carefully   4._____
5. ability   5._____
6. temper   6._____
7. deslike   7._____
8. seldem   8._____
9. alcohol   9._____
10. expense   10._____
11. vegatable   11._____
12. dispensary   12._____
13. specemin   13._____
14. allowance   14._____
15. exersise   15._____

KEY (CORRECT ANSWERS)

1.	W	6.	C	11.	W
2.	W	7.	W	12.	C
3.	C	8.	W	13.	W
4.	C	9.	C	14.	C
5.	C	10.	C	15.	W

TEST 10

DIRECTIONS: Each of Questions 1 through 10 consists of four words, one of which may be spelled incorrectly or all four words may be spelled correctly. If one of the words in a question is spelled incorrectly, print in the space at the right the capital letter preceding the word which is spelled INCORRECTLY. If all four words are spelled CORRECTLY, print the letter E.

1. A. dismissal   B. collateral   1.____
   C. leisure   D. proffession

2. A. subsidary   B. outrageous   2.____
   C. liaison   D. assessed

3. A. already   B. changeable   3.____
   C. mischevous   D. cylinder

4. A. supersede   B. deceit   4.____
   C. dissension   D. imminent

5. A. arguing   B. contagious   5.____
   C. comparitive   D. accessible

6. A. indelible   B. existance   6.____
   C. presumptuous   D. mileage

7. A. extention   B. aggregate   7.____
   C. sustenance   D. gratuitous

8. A. interrogate   B. exaggeration   8.____
   C. vacillate   D. moreover

9. A. parallel   B. derogatory   9.____
   C. admissible   D. appellate

10. A. safety   B. cumalative   10.____
    C. disappear   D. usable

KEY (CORRECT ANSWERS)

1.	D	6.	B
2.	A	7.	A
3.	C	8.	E
4.	E	9.	C
5.	C	10.	B

TEST 11

DIRECTIONS: Each of questions 1 through 10 consists of four words, one of which may be spelled incorrectly or all four words may be spelled correctly. If one of the words in a question is spelled INCORRECTLY, print in the space at the right the capital letter preceding the word which is spelled incorrectly. If all four words are spelled CORRECTLY, print the letter E.

1. A. vehicular B. gesticulate 1._____
   C. manageable D. fullfil

2. A. inovation B. onerous 2._____
   C. chastise D. irresistible

3. A. familiarize B. dissolution 3._____
   C. oscillate D. superflous

4. A. census B. defender 4._____
   C. adherence D. inconceivable

5. A. voluminous B. liberalize 5._____
   C. bankrupcy D. conversion

6. A. justifiable B. executor 6._____
   C. perpatrate D. dispelled

7. A. boycott B. abeyence 7._____
   C. enterprise D. circular

8. A. spontaineous B. dubious 8._____
   C. analyze D. premonition

9. A. intelligible B. apparently 9._____
   C. genuine D. crucial

10. A. plentiful B. ascertain 10._____
    C. carreer D. preliminary

KEY (CORRECT ANSWERS)

1.	D	6.	C
2.	A	7.	B
3.	D	8.	A
4.	E	9.	E
5.	C	10.	C

TEST 12

DIRECTIONS: Each of questions 1 through 25 consists of four words, one of which may be spelled incorrectly or all four words may be spelled correctly. If one of the words in a question is spelled INCORRECTLY, print in the space at the right the capital letter preceding the word which is spelled incorrectly. If all four words are spelled CORRECTLY, print the letter E.

1. A. temporary   B. existance   1.____
   C. complimentary   D. altogether

2. A. privilege   B. changeable   2.____
   C. jeopardize   D. commitment

3. A. grievous   B. alloted   3.____
   C. outrageous   D. mortgage

4. A. tempermental   B. accommodating   4.____
   C. bookkeeping   D. panicky

5. A. auxiliary   B. indispensable   5.____
   C. ecstasy   D. fiery

6. A. dissappear   B. buoyant   6.____
   C. imminent   D. parallel

7. A. loosly   B. medicine   7.____
   C. schedule   D. defendant

8. A. endeavor   B. persuade   8.____
   C. retroactive   D. desparate

9. A. usage   B. servicable   9.____
   C. disadvantageous   D. remittance

10. A. beneficary   B. receipt   10.____
    C. excitable   D. implement

11. A. accompanying   B. intangible   11.____
    C. offered   D. movable

12. A. controlling   B. seize   12.____
    C. repetitious   D. miscellaneous

13. A. installation   B. accommodation   13.____
    C. consistant   D. illuminate

14. A. incidentaly   B. privilege   14.____
    C. apparent   D. chargeable

122

2 (#12)

15. A. prevalent B. serial 15.____
    C. briefly D. disatisfied

16. A. reciprocal B. concurrence 16.____
    C. persistence D. withold

17. A. deferred B. suing 17.____
    C. fulfilled D. pursuant

18. A. questionable B. omission 18.____
    C. acknowledgment D. insistent

19. A. guarantee B. committment 19.____
    C. mitigate D. publicly

20. A. prerogative B. apprise 20.____
    C. extrordinary D. continual

21. A. arrogant B. handicapped 21.____
    C. judicious D. perennial

22. A. permissable B. deceive 22.____
    C. innumerable D. retrieve

23. A. notable B. allegiance 23.____
    C. reimburse D. illegal

24. A. wholly B. disbursement 24.____
    C. hindrance D. conciliatory

25. A. guidance B. condemn 25.____
    C. publically D. coercion

KEY (CORRECT ANSWERS)

1.	B		11.	C
2.	E		12.	E
3.	B		13.	C
4.	A		14.	A
5.	E		15.	D
6.	A		16.	D
7.	A		17.	E
8.	D		18.	A
9.	B		19.	B
10.	A		20.	C

21. E
22. A
23. E
24. E
25. C

FILING
EXAMINATION SECTION
TEST 1

Questions 1-9.

DIRECTIONS: An important part of the duties of an office worker in a public agency is to file office records. Questions 1 through 9 are designed to determine whether you can file records correctly. Each of these questions consists of four names. For each question, select the one of the four names that should be FOURTH if the four names were arranged in alphabetical order. *PRINT THE LETTER OF THE CORRECT ANSWER IN THE SPACE AT THE RIGHT.*

1. A. 6th National Bank B. Sexton Lock Co. 1.____
   C. The 69th Street League D. Thomas Saxon Corp.

2. A. 4th Avenue Printing Co. B. The Four Corners Corp. 2.____
   C. Dr. Milton Fournet D. The Martin Fountaine Co.

3. A. Mr. Chas. Le Mond B. Model Express, Inc. 3.____
   C. Lenox Enterprises D. Mobile Supply Co.

4. A. Frank Waller Johnson B. Frank Walter Johnson 4.____
   C. Wilson Johnson D. Frank W. Johnson

5. A. Miss Anne M. Carlsen B. Mrs. Albert S. Carlson 5.____
   C. Mr. Alan Ross Carlsen D. Dr. Anthony Ash Carlson

6. A. Delaware Paper Co. B. William Del Ville 6.____
   C. Ralph A. Delmar D. Wm. K. Del Ville

7. A. The Lloyd Disney Co. B. Mrs. Raymond Norris 7.____
   C. Oklahoma Envelope, Inc. D. Miss Esther O'Neill

8. A. The Olympic Eraser Co. B. Mrs. Raymond Norris 8.____
   C. Oklahoma Envelope, Inc. D. Miss Esther O'Neill

9. A. Patricia MacNamara B. Eleanor McNally 9.____
   C. Robt. MacPherson, Jr. D. Helen McNair

Questions 10-21.

DIRECTIONS: Questions 10 through 21 are to be answered on the basis of the usual rules for alphabetical filing. For each question, indicate in the space at the right the letter preceding the name which should be THIRD in alphabetical order.

2 (#1)

10. A. Russell Cohen B. Henry Cohn 10.____
    C. Wesley Chambers D. Arthur Connors

11. A. Wanda Jenkins B. Pauline Jennings 11.____
    C. Leslie Jantzenberg D. Rudy Jensen

12. A. Arnold Wilson B. Carlton Willson 12.____
    C. Duncan Williamson D. Ezra Wilston

13. A. Joseph M. Buchman B. Gustave Bozzerman 13.____
    C. Constantino Brunelli D. Armando Buccino

14. A. Barbara Waverly B. Corinne Warterdam 14.____
    C. Dennis Waterman D. Harold Wartman

15. A. Jose Mejia B. Bernard Mendelsohn 15.____
    C. Antonio Mejias D. Richard Mazzitelli

16. A. Hesselberg, Norman J. B. Hesselman, Nathan B. 16.____
    C. Hazel, Robert S. D. Heintz, August J.

17. A. Oshins, Jerome B. Ohsie, Marjorie 17.____
    C. O'Shaugn, F.J. D. O'Shea, Frances

18. A. Petrie, Joshua A. B. Pendleton, Oscar 18.____
    C. Pertwee, Joshua D. Perkins, Warren G.

19. A. Morganstern, Alfred B. Morganstern, Albert 19.____
    C. Monroe, Mildred D. Modesti, Ernest

20. A. More, Stewart B. Moorhead, Jay 20.____
    C. Moore, Benjamin D. Moffat, Edith

21. A. Ramirez, Paul B. Revere, Pauline 21.____
    C. Ramos, Felix D. Ramazotti, Angelo

KEY (CORRECT ANSWERS)

1.	C	11.	B
2.	A	12.	A
3.	B	13.	D
4.	B	14.	C
5.	D	15.	C
6.	A	16.	A
7.	C	17.	D
8.	D	18.	C
9.	B	19.	B
10.	B	20.	B

21. C

TEST 2

DIRECTIONS: Each question or incomplete statement is followed by several suggested answers or completions. Select the one that BEST answers the question or completes the statement. *PRINT THE LETTER OF THE CORRECT ANSWER IN THE SPACE AT THE RIGHT.*

Questions 1-4.

DIRECTIONS: Questions 1 through 4 are to be answered on the basis of the following alphabetical rules.

RULES FOR ALPHABETICAL FILING

Names of Individuals

The names of individuals are filed in strict alphabetical order, *first* according to the last name, *then* according to first name or initial, and *finally* according to middle name or initial. For example: George Allen precedes Edward Bell and Leonard Reston precedes Lucille Reston.

When last names are the same, for example, A. Green and Agnes Green, the one with the initial comes before the one with the name written out when the first initials are identical.

Prefixes such as De, O', Mac, Mc and Van are filed as written and are treated as part of the names to which they are connected. For example, Gladys McTeaque is filed before Frances Meadows.

1. If the following four names were put into an alphabetical list, what would the FIRST name on the list be? 1.____
    A. Wm. C. Paul B. W. Paul
    C. Alice Paul D. Alyce Paule

2. If the following four names were put into an alphabetical list, what would the THIRD name on the list be? 2.____
    A. I. MacCarthy B. Irene MacKarthy
    C. Ida McCaren D. I.A. McCarthy

3. If the following four names were put into an alphabetical list, what would the SECOND name on the list be? 3.____
    A. John Gilhooley B. Ramon Gonzalez
    C. Gerald Gilholy D. Samuel Gilvecchio

4. If the following four names were put into an alphabetical list, what would the FOURTH name on the list be? 4.____
    A. Michael Edwinn B. James Edwards
    C. Mary Edwin D. Carlo Edwards

Questions 5-9.

DIRECTIONS: Questions 5 through 9 consist of a group of names which are to be arranged in alphabetical order for filing.

5. Of the following, the name which should be filed FIRST is
   A. Joseph J. Meadeen
   B. Gerard L. Meader
   C. John F. Madcar
   D. Philip F. Malder

6. Of the following, the name which should be filed LAST is
   A. Stephen Fischer
   B. Benjamin Fitchmann
   C. Thomas Fishman
   D. Augustus S. Fisher

7. The name which should be filed SECOND is
   A. Yeatman, Frances
   B. Yeaton, C.S.
   C. Yeatman, R.M.
   D. Yeats, John

8. The name which should be filed THIRD is
   A. Hauser, Ann
   B. Hauptmann, Jane
   C. Hauster, Mary
   D. Rauprich, Julia

9. The name which should be filed SECOND is
   A. Flora McDougall
   B. Fred E. MacDowell
   C. Juanita Mendez
   D. James A. Madden

Questions 10-14.

DIRECTIONS: Questions 10 through 14 are to be answered based on an alphabetical arrangement of the following list of names.

Walker, Carol J.	Wacht, Michael	Wade, Ethel
Wall, Fredrick	Wall, Francis	Wall, Frank
Wachs, Paul	Walker, Carol L.	Wagner, Arthur
Walters, Daniel	Wade, Ellen	Wald, William
Wagner, Allen	Walters, David	Walker, Carmen

10. The 4th name on the alphabetized list would be
    A. Wade, Ellen
    B. Wade, Ethel
    C. Wagner, Allen
    D. Wagner, Arthur

11. The 7th name on the alphabetized list would be
    A. Walker, Carmen
    B. Walker, Carol J.
    C. Walker, Carol L.
    D. Wald, William

12. The name that would come immediately AFTER Wagner, Arthur on the alphabetized list would be
    A. Wade, Ethel
    B. Wagner, Allen
    C. Wald, William
    D. Walker, Carol L.

13. The name that would come immediately BEFORE Wall, Frank would be 13.____
    A. Wall, Francis
    B. Wall, Fredrick
    C. Walters, David
    D. Walters, Daniel

14. The 12th name on the alphabetized list would be 14.____
    A. Walker, Carol L.
    B. Wald, William
    C. Wall, Francis
    D. Wall, Frank

KEY (CORRECT ANSWERS)

1.	C	6.	B	11.	D
2.	C	7.	C	12.	C
3.	A	8.	A	13.	A
4.	A	9.	D	14.	D
5.	C	10.	B		

TEST 3

DIRECTIONS: Each question or incomplete statement is followed by several suggested answers or completions. Select the one that BEST answers the question or completes the statement. *PRINT THE LETTER OF THE CORRECT ANSWER IN THE SPACE AT THE RIGHT.*

Questions 1-8.

DIRECTIONS: Questions 1 through 8 are based on the Rules of Alphabetical Filing given below. Read these rules carefully before answering the questions.

Names of People
1. The names of people are filed in strict alphabetical order, first according to the last name, then according to first name or initial, and finally according to middle name or initial. For example: George Allen comes before Edward Bell, and Leonard P. Reston comes before Lucille B. Reston.

2. When last names are the same, for example, A. Green and Agnes Green, the one with the initial comes before the one with the name written out when the first initials are identical.

3. When first and last names are alike and the middle name is given, for example, John David Doe and John Devoe Doe, the names should be filed in alphabetical order of the middle names.

4. When first and last names are the same, a name without a middle initial comes before one with a middle name or initial. For example, John Doe comes before John A. Doe and John Alan Doe.

5. When first and last names are the same, a name with a middle initial comes before one with a middle name beginning with the same initial. For example, Jack R. Hertz comes before Jack Richard Hertz.

6. Prefixes such as De, O', Mac, Mc, and Van are filed as written and are treated as part of the names to which they are connected. For example, Robert O'Dea is filed before David Olsen.

7. Abbreviated names are treated as if they were spelled out. For example: Chas. is filed as Charles and Thos. is filed as Thomas.

8. Titles and designations such as Dr., Mr., and Prof. are disregarded in filing.

Names of Organizations
1. The names of business organizations are filed according to the order in which each word in the name appears. When an organization name bears the name of a person, it is filed according to the rules for filing names of people as given above. For example: William Smith Service Co. comes before Television Distributors, Inc.

2. Where bureau, board, office or department appears as the first part of the title of a governmental agency, that agency should be filed under the word in the title expressing the chief function of the agency. For example, Bureau of Budget would be filed as if written Budget, (Bureau of the). The Department of Personnel would be filed as if written Personnel, (Department of).

3. When the following words are part of an organization, they are disregarded: the, of, and.

4. When there are numbers in a name, they are treated as if they were spelled out. For example: 10th Street Bootery is filed as Tenth Street Bootery.

Each question from 1 through 8 contains four names numbered from 1 through 4 but not necessarily numbered in correct filing order. Answer each question by choosing the letter corresponding to the CORRECT filing order of the four names in accordance with the above rules.

SAMPLE QUESTION:
I. Robert J. Smith
II. R. Jeffrey Smith
III. Dr. A. Smythe
IV. Allen R. Smithers

A. I, II, III, IV   B. III, I, II, IV   C. II, I, IV, III   D. III, II, I, IV

Since the correct filing order, in accordance with the above rules is II I, IV, III, the correct answer is C.

1. I. J. Chester VanClief   II. John C. Van Clief
    III. J. VanCleve   IV. Mary L. Vance

    The CORRECT answer is:
    A. IV, III, I, II   B. IV, III, II, I   C. III, I, II, IV   D. III, IV, I, II

2. I. Community Development Agency   II. Department of Social Services
    III. Board of Estimate   IV. Bureau of Gas and Electricity

    The CORRECT answer is:
    A. III, IV, I, II   B. 1, II, IV, III   C. II, I, III, IV   D. I, III, IV, II

3. I. Dr. Chas. K. Dahlman   II. F. & A. Delivery Service
    III. Department of Water Supply   IV. Demano Men's Custom Tailors

    The CORRECT answer is:
    A. I, II, III, IV   B. I, IV, II, III   C. IV, I, II, III   D. IV, I, III, II

4. I.   48th Street Theater   II. Fourteenth Street Day Care Center   4._____
    III. Professor A. Cartwright   IV. Albert F. McCarthy

    The CORRECT answer is:
       A. IV, II, I, III   B. IV, III, I, II   C. III, II, I, IV   D. III, I, II, IV

5. I.   Frances D'Arcy   II. Mario L. DelAmato   5._____
    III. William R. Diamond   IV. Robert J. DuBarry

    The CORRECT answer is:
       A. I, II, IV, III   B. II, I, III, IV   C. I, II, III, IV   D. II, I, III, IV

6. I.   Evelyn H. D'Amelio   II. Jane R. Bailey   6._____
    III. Robert Bailey   IV. Frank Baily

    The CORRECT answer is:
       A. I, II, III, IV   B. I, III, II, IV   C. II, III, IV, I   D. III, II, IV, I

7. I.   Department of Markets   7._____
    II. Bureau of Handicapped Children
    III. Housing Authority Administration Building
    IV. Board of Pharmacy

    The CORRECT answer is:
       A. II, I, III, IV   B. I, II, IV, III   C. I, II, III, IV   D. III, II, I, IV

8. I.   William A. Shea Stadium   II. Rapid Speed Taxi Co.   8._____
    III. Harry Stampler's Rotisserie III. Wilhelm Albert Shea

    The CORRECT answer is:
       A. II, III, IV, I   B. IV, I, III, II   C. II, IV, I, III   D. III, IV, I, II

Questions 9-18.

DIRECTIONS: Questions 9 through 18 each show in Column I names written on four ledger cards (lettered w, x, y, z) which have to be filed. You are to choose the option (lettered A, B, C, or D) in Column II which BEST represents the proper order for filing the cards.

SAMPLE

COLUMN I		COLUMN II
w.	John Stevens	A. w, y, z, x
x.	John D. Stevenson	B. y, w, z, x
y.	Joan Stevens	C. x, y, w, z
z.	J. Stevenson	D. x, w, y, z

The correct way to file the cards is:
y. Joan Stevens
w. John Stevens
z. J. Stevenson
x. John D. Stevenson

The correct order is shown by the letters y, w, z, x in that sequence. Since, in Column II, B appears in front of the letters y, w, z, x in that sequence, B is the correct answer to the sample question.

Now answer the following questions, using the same procedure.

9. COLUMN I
   w. Juan Montoya
   x. Manuel Montenegro
   y. Victor Matos
   z. Victoria Maltos

   COLUMN II
   A. y, z, x, w
   B. z, y, x, w
   C. z, y, w, x
   D. y, x, z, w

   9.____

10. COLUMN I
    w. Frank Carlson
    x. Robert Carlson
    y. George Carlson
    z. Frank Carlton

    COLUMN II
    A. z, x, w, y
    B. z, y, x, w
    C. w, y, z, x
    D. w, z, y, x

    10.____

11. COLUMN I
    w. Carmine Rivera
    x. Jose Rivera
    y. Frank River
    z. Joan Rivers

    COLUMN II
    A. y, w, x, z
    B. y, x, w, z
    C. w, x, y, z
    D. w, x, z, y

    11.____

12. COLUMN I
    w. Jerome Mathews
    x. Scott A. Matthew
    y. Charles B. Matthew
    z. Scott C. Mathewsw

    COLUMN II
    A. w, y, z, x
    B. z, y, x, w
    C. z, w, x, y
    D. w, z, y, x

    12.____

13. COLUMN I
    w. John McMahan
    x. John P. MacMahan
    y. Joseph DeMayo
    z. Joseph D. Mayo

    COLUMN II
    A. w, x, y, z
    B. y, x, z, w
    C. x, w, y, z
    D. y, x, w, z

    13.____

14. COLUMN I
    w. Raymond Martinez
    x. Ramon Martinez
    y. Prof. Ray Martinez
    z. Dr. Raymond Martin

    COLUMN II
    A. z, x, y, w
    B. z, y, x, w
    C. z, w, y, x
    D. y, x, w, z

    14.____

4 (#3)

15. COLUMN I
    w. Mr. Robert Vincent Mackintosh
    x. Robert Reginald Macintosh
    y. Roger V. McIntosh
    z. Robert R. Mackintosh

    COLUMN II
    A. y, x, z, w
    B. x, w, z, y
    C. x, w, y, z
    D. x, z, w, y

    15.____

16. COLUMN I
    w. Dr. D. V. Facsone
    x. Prof. David Fascone
    y. Donald Facsone
    z. Mrs. D. Fascone

    COLUMN II
    A. y, w, z, x
    B. w, y, x, z
    C. w, y, z, x
    D. z, w, x, y

    16.____

17. COLUMN I
    w. Johnathan Q. Addams
    x. John Quincy Adams
    y. J. Quincy Addams
    z. Jerimiah Adams

    COLUMN II
    A. z, x, w, y
    B. z, x, y, w
    C. y, w, x, z
    D. x, w, z, y

    17.____

18. COLUMN I
    w. Nehimiah Persoff
    x. Newton Pershing
    y. Newman Perring
    z. Nelson Persons

    COLUMN II
    A. w, z, x, y
    B. x, z, y, w
    C. y, x, w, z
    D. z, y, w, x

    18.____

KEY (CORRECT ANSWERS)

1.	A	6.	D	11.	A	16.	C
2.	D	7.	D	12.	D	17.	B
3.	B	8.	C	13.	B	18.	C
4.	D	9.	B	14.	A		
5.	C	10.	C	15.	D		

TEST 4

Questions 1-13.

DIRECTIONS: Each question from 1 through 13 contains four names. For each question, choose the name that should be FIRST if he four names are to be arranged in alphabetical order in accordance with the Rule for Alphabetical Filing of Names of People given below. Read this rule carefully. Then, for each question, mark your answer space with the letter that is next to the name that should be first in alphabetical order.

RULE FOR ALPHABETICAL FILING OF NAMES OF PEOPLE

The names of people are filed in strict alphabetical order, first according to the last name, then according to the first name. For example; George Allen comes before Edward Bell, and Alice Reston comes before Lucille Reston.

SAMPLE QUESTION
A. Roger Smith (2)
B. Joan Smythe (4)
C. Alan Smith (1)
D. James Smithe (3)

The number in parentheses show the proper alphabetical order in which these names should be filed. Since the name that should be filed FIRST is Alan Smith, the correct answer to the sample question is C.

1. A. William Claremont   B. Antonio Clements
   C. Anthony Clemente   D. William Claymont

2. A. Wayne Fumando   B. Sarah Femando
   C. Susan Fumando   D. Wilson Femando

3. A. Wilbur Hanson   B. Wm. Hansen
   C. Robert Hansen   D. Thomas Hanson

4. A. George St. John   B. Thomas Santos
   C. Frances Starks   D. Mary S. Stranum

5. A. Franklin Carrol   B. Timothy Carrol
   C. Timothy S. Carol   D. Frank F. Carroll

6. A. Christie-Barry Storage   B. John Christie-Barry
   C. The Christie-Barry Company   D. Anne Christie-Barrie

7. A. Inter State Travel Co.   A. Interstate Car Rental
   C. Inter State Trucking   D. Interstate Lending Inst.

2 (#4)

8. A. The Los Angeles Tile Co. 8.____
   B. Anita F. Los
   C. The Lost & Found Detective Agency
   D. Jason Los-Brio

9. A. Prince Charles   B. Prince Charles Coiffures   9.____
   C. Chas. F. Prince   D. Thomas A. Charles

10. A. U.S. Dept. of Agriculture   B. United States Aircraft Co. 10.____
    C. U.S. Air Transport, Inc.   D. The United Union

11. A. Meyer's Art Shop   B. Frank B. Meyer   11.____
    C. Meyers' Paint Store   D. Meyer and Goldberg

12. A. David Des Laurier   B. Des Moines Flower Shop   12.____
    C. Henry Desanto   D. Mary L. Desta

13. A. Jeffrey Van Der Meer   B. Jeffrey M. Vander   13.____
    C. Jeffrey Van   D. Wallace Meer

KEY (CORRECT ANSWERS)

1.	A	6.	D	11.	A
2.	B	7.	B	12.	C
3.	C	8.	B	13.	D
4.	A	9.	D		
5.	C	10.	C		

TEST 5

Questions 1-10.

DIRECTIONS: Questions 1 through 10 are to be answered on the basis of the usual rules of filing. Column I lists, next to the numbers 1 to 10, the names of 10 clinic patients. Column II lists, next to the letters A to D, the headings of file drawers into which you are to place the records of these patients. For each question, indicate in the space at the right the letter preceding the heading of the file drawer in which the record should be filed.

	COLUMN I		COLUMN II	
1.	Charles Coughlin	A.	Cab-Cep	1.____
2.	Mary Carstairs	B.	Ceq-Cho	2.____
3.	Joseph Collin	C.	Chr-Coj	3.____
4.	Thomas Chelsey	D.	Cok-Czy	4.____
5.	Cedric Chalmers			5.____
6.	Mae Clarke			6.____
7.	Dora Copperhead			7.____
8.	Arnold Cohn			8.____
9.	Charlotte Crumboldt			9.____
10.	Frances Celine			10.____

Questions 11-18.

DIRECTIONS: Questions 11 to 18 are to be answered on the basis of the usual rules of filing. Column I lists, next to the numbers 11 to 18, the names of 8 clinic patients. Column II lists, next to the letters A to O, the headings of file drawers into which you are to place the records of these patients. For each question, indicate in the space at the right the letter preceding the heading of the file drawer in which the record should be filed.

2 (#5)

COLUMN I	COLUMN II	
11. Thomas Adams	A. Aab-Abi	11._____
	B. Abj-Ach	
12. Joseph Albert	C. Aci-Aco	12._____
	D. Acp-Ada	
13. Frank Anaster	E. Adb-Afr	13._____
	F. Afs-Ago	
14. Charles Abt	G. Agp-Ahz	14._____
	H. Aia-Ako	
15. John Alfred	I. Akp-Ald	15._____
	J. Ale-Amo	
16. Louis Aron	K. Amp-Aor	16._____
	L. Aos-Apr	
17. Francis Amos	M. Aps-Asi	17._____
	N. Asj-Ati	
18. William Adler	O. Atj-Awz	18._____

Questions 19-28.

DIRECTIONS: Questions 19 through 28 are to be answered on the basis of the usual rules of filing. Column I lists, next to the numbers 19 through 28, the names of 10 clinic patients. Column II lists, next to the letters A to D the headings of file drawers into which you are to place the medical records of these patients. For each question, indicate in the space at the right the letter preceding the heading of the file drawer in which the record should be filed.

COLUMN I	COLUMN II	
19. Frank Shea	A. Sab-Sej	19._____
20. Rose Seaborn	B. Sek-Sio	20._____
21. Samuel Smollin	C. Sip-Soo	21._____
22. Thomas Shur	D. Sop-Syz	22._____
23. Ben Schaefer		23._____
24. Shirley Strauss		24._____
25. Harry Spiro		25._____
26. Dora Skelly		26._____
27. Sylvia Smith		27._____
28. Arnold Selz		28._____

KEY (CORRECT ANSWERS)

1.	D	11.	D	21.	C
2.	A	12.	I	22.	B
3.	D	13.	K	23.	A
4.	B	14.	B	24.	D
5.	B	15.	J	25.	D
6.	C	16.	M	26.	C
7.	D	17.	J	27.	C
8.	C	18.	E	28.	B
9.	D	19.	B		
10.	A	20.	A		

NAME AND NUMBER CHECKING
EXAMINATION SECTION
TEST 1

DIRECTIONS: Questions 1 through 17 consist of sets of names and addresses. In each question, the name and address in Column II should be an exact copy of the name and address in Column I.
If there is:
a mistake only in the name, mark your answer A;
a mistake only in the address, mark your answer B;
a mistake in both name and address, mark your answer C;
No mistake in either name or address, mark your answer D.

Sample Question

Column I	Column II
Christina Magnusson	Christina Magnusson
288 Greene Street	288 Greene Street
New York, N.Y. 10003	New York, N.Y. 10013

Since there is a mistake only in the address (the zip code should be 10003 instead of 10013), the answer to the sample question is B.

	COLUMN I	COLUMN II	
1.	Ms. Joan Kelly 313 Franklin Avenue Brooklyn, N.Y. 11202	Ms. Joan Kielly 318 Franklin Ave. Brooklyn, N.Y. 11202	1.____
2.	Mrs. Eileen Engel 47-24 86 Road Queens, N.Y. 11122	Mrs. Ellen Engel 47-24 86 Road Queens, New York 11122	2.____
3.	Marcia Michaels 213 E. 81 St. New York, N.Y. 10012	Marcia Michaels 213 E. 81 St. New York, N.Y. 10012	3.____
4.	Rev. Edward J. Smyth 1401 Brandeis Street San Francisco, Calif. 96201	Rev. Edward J. Smyth 1401 Brandies Street San Francisco, Calif. 96201	4.____
5.	Alicia Rodriguez 24-68 82 St. Elmhurst, N.Y. 11122	Alicia Rodriguez 2468 81 St. Elmhurst, N.Y. 11122	5.____

2 (#1)

COLUMN I	COLUMN II	
6. Ernest Eisemann 21 Columbia St. New York, N.Y. 10007	Ernest Eisermann 21 Columbia St. New York, N.Y. 10007	6.____
7. Mr. & Mrs. George Petersson 87-11 91st Avenue Woodhaven, N.Y. 11421	Mr. & Mrs. George Peterson 87-11 91st Avenue Woodhaven, N.Y. 11421	7.____
8. Mr. Ivan Klebnikov 1848 Newkirk Avenue Brooklyn, N.Y. 11226	Mr. Ivan Klebikov 1848 Newkirk Avenue Brooklyn, N.Y. 11622	8.____
9. Mr. Samuel Rothfleisch 71 Pine Street New York, N.Y. 10005	Samuel Rothfleisch 71 Pine Street New York, N.Y. 100005	9.____
10. Mrs. Isabel Tonnessen 198 East 185th Street Bronx, N.Y. 10458	Mrs. Isabel Tonnessen 189 East 185th Street Bronx, N.Y. 10348	10.____
11. Esteban Perez 173 Eighth Street Staten Island, N.Y. 10306	Estaban Perez 173 Eighth Street Staten Island, N.Y. 10306	11.____
12. Esta Wong 141 West 68 St. New York, N.Y. 10023	Esta Wang 141 West 68 St. New York, N.Y. 10023	12.____
13. Dr. Alberto Grosso 3475 12th Avenue Brooklyn, N.Y. 11218	Dr. Alberto Grosso 3475 12th Avenue Brooklyn, N.Y. 11218	13.____
14. Mrs. Ruth Bortias 482 Theresa Ct. Far Rockaway, N.Y. 11691	Ms. Ruth Bortlas 482 Theresa Ct. Far Rockaway, N.Y. 11169	14.____
15. Mr. & Mrs. Howard Fox 2301 Sedgwick Ave. Bronx, N.Y. 10468	Mr. & Mrs. Howard Fox 231 Sedgwick Ave. Bronx, N.Y. 10468	15.____
16. Miss Marjorie Black 223 East 23 Street New York, N.Y. 10010	Miss Margorie Black 223 East 23 Street New York, N.Y. 10010	16.____

3 (#1)

COLUMN I	COLUMN II	
17. Michelle Herman 806 Valley Rd. Old Tappan, N.J. 07675	Michelle Hermann 806 Valley Dr. Old Tappan, N.J. 07675	17.____

KEY (CORRECT ANSWERS)

1.	C	7.	A	13.	D
2.	A	8.	C	14.	C
3.	D	9.	D	15.	B
4.	B	10.	B	16.	A
5.	B	11.	A	17.	C
6.	A	12.	D		

TEST 2

DIRECTIONS: Questions 1 through 15 are to be answered SOLELY on the instructions given below. *PRINT THE LETTER OF THE CORRECT ANSWER IN THE SPACE AT THE RIGHT.*

INSTRUCTIONS

In each of the following questions, the 3-line name and address in Column I is the master-list entry, and the 3-line entry in Column II is the information to be checked against the master list. If there is one line that does not match, mark your answer A; if there are two lines that do not match, mark your answer B; if all three lines do not match, mark your answer C; if the lines all match exactly, mark your answer D.

Sample Question

Column I
Mark L. Field
11-09 Price Park Blvd.
Bronx, N.Y. 11402

Column II
Mark L. Field
11-99 Prince Park Way
Bronx, N.Y. 11401

The first lines in each column match exactly. The second lines do not match since 11-09 does not match 11-<u>99</u>; and Blvd. does not match <u>Way</u>. The third lines do not match either since 11<u>402</u> does not match 11<u>401</u>. Therefore, there are two lines that do not match, and the CORRECT answer is B.

COLUMN I

1. Jerome A. Jackson
   1243 14th Avenue
   New York, N.Y. 10023

2. Sophie Strachtheim
   33-28 Connecticut Ave.
   Far Rockaway, N.Y. 11697

3. Elisabeth N.T. Gorrell
   256 Exchange St.
   New York, N.Y. 10013

4. Maria J. Gonzalez
   7516 E. Sheepshead Rd.
   Brooklyn, N.Y. 11240

5. Leslie B. Brautenweiler
   21 57A Seiler Terr.
   Flushing, N.Y. 11367

COLUMN II

Jerome A. Johnson
1234 14th Avenue
New York, N.Y. 10023

Sophie Strachtheim
33-28 Connecticut Ave.
Far Rockaway, N.Y. 11697

Elizabeth N.T. Gorrell
256 Exchange St.
New York, N.Y. 10013

Maria J. Gonzalez
7516 N. Shepshead Rd.
Brooklyn, N.Y. 11240

Leslie B. Brautenwieler
21-75A Seiler Terr.
Flushing, N.J. 11367

1._____

2._____

3._____

4._____

5._____

2 (#2)

COLUMN I	COLUMN II	
6. Rigoberto J. Peredes 157 Twin Towers, #18F Tottenville, S. I., N.Y,	Rigoberto J. Peredes 157 Twin Towers, #18F Tottenville, S.I., N.Y.	6.____
7. Pietro F. Albino P.O. Box 7548 Floral Park, N.Y. 11005	Pietro F. Albina P.O. Box 7458 Floral Park, N.Y. 11005	7.____
8. Joanne Zimmerman Bldg. SW, Room 314 532-4601	Joanne Zimmermann Bldg. SW, Room 314 532-4601	8.____
9. Carlyle Whetstone Payroll Div. –A, Room 212A 262-5000, ext. 471	Carlyle Whetstone Payroll Div. –A, Room 212A 262-5000, ext. 417	9.____
10. Kenneth Chiang Legal Council, Room 9745 (201) 416-9100, ext. 17	Kenneth Chiang Legal Counsel, Room 9745 (201) 416-9100, Ext. 17	10.____
11. Ethel Koenig Personnel Services Division, Room 433; 635-7572	Ethel Hoenig Personal Services Division, Room 433; 635-7527	11.____
12. Joyce Ehrhardt Office of the Administrator, Room W56; 387-8706	Joyce Ehrhart Office of the Administrator, Room W56; 387-7806	12.____
13. Ruth Lang EAM Bldg., Room C101 625-2000, ext. 765	Ruth Lang EAM Bldg., Room C110 625-2000, ext. 765	13.____
14. Anne Marie Ionozzi Investigations, Room 827 576-4000, ext. 832	Anna Marie Ionozzi Investigation, Room 827 566-4000, ext. 832	14.____
15. Willard Jameson Fm C Bldg., Room 687 454-3010	Willard Jamieson Fm C Bldg., Room 687 454-3010	15.____

KEY (CORRECT ANSWERS)

1.	B	6.	D		C
2.	D	7.	B	12.	B
3.	A	8.	D	13.	A
4.	A	9.	B	14.	C
5.	C	10.	A	15.	A

TEST 3

DIRECTIONS: Questions 1 through 10 are to be answered on the basis of the following instructions. *PRINT THE LETTER OF THE CORRECT ANSWER IN THE SPACE AT THE RIGHT.*

INSTRUCTIONS
For each such set of names, addresses, and numbers listed in Columns I and II, select your answer from the following options:
The names in Columns I and II are different,
The addresses in Columns I and II are different,
The numbers in Columns I and II are different,
The names, addresses, and numbers in Columns I and II are identical.

COLUMN I	COLUMN II	
1. Francis Jones 62 Stately Avenue 96-12446	Francis Jones 62 Stately Avenue 96-21446	1.____
2. Julio Montez 19 Ponderosa Road 56-73161	Julio Montez 19 Ponderosa Road 56-71361	2.____
3. Mary Mitchell 2314 Melbourne Drive 68-92172	Mary Mitchell 2314 Melbourne Drive 68-92172	3.____
4. Harry Patterson 25 Dunne Street 14-33430	Harry Patterson 25 Dunne Street 14-34330	4.____
5. Patrick Murphy 171 West Hosmer Street 93-81214	Patrick Murphy 171 West Hosmer Street 93-18214	5.____
6. August Schultz 816 St. Clair Avenue 53-40149	August Schultz 816 St. Claire Avenue 53-40149	6.____
7. George Taft 72 Runnymede Street 47-04033	George Taft 72 Runnymede Street 47-04023	7.____
8. Angus Henderson 1418 Madison Street 81-76375	Angus Henderson 1318 Madison Street 81-76375	8.____

2 (#3)

COLUMN I	COLUMN II	
9. Carolyn Mazur 12 Riverview Road 38-99615	Carolyn Mazur 12 Rivervane Road 38-99615	9.____
10. Adele Russell 1725 Lansing Lane 72-91962	Adela Russell 1725 Lansing Lane 72-91962	10.____

KEY (CORRECT ANSWERS)

1.	C	6.	B
2.	C	7.	C
3.	D	8.	D
4.	C	9.	B
5.	C	10.	A

TEST 4

DIRECTIONS: Questions 1 through 20 test how good you are at catching mistakes in typing or printing. In each question, the name and address in Column II should be an exact copy of the name and address in Column I. Mark your answer
  A. If there is no mistake in either name or address;
  B. If there is a mistake in both name and address;
  C. If there is a mistake only in the name;
  D. If there is a mistake only in the address.
PRINT THE LETTER OF THE CORRECT ANSWER IN THE SPACE AT THE RIGHT.

COLUMN I | COLUMN II

1. Milos Yanocek
   33-60 14 Street
   Long Island City, N.Y. 11011

   Milos Yanocek
   33-60 14 Street
   Long Island City, N.Y. 11001

   1.____

2. Alphonse Sabattelo
   24 Minnetta Lane
   New York, N.Y. 10006

   Alphonse Sabbattelo
   24 Minetta Lane
   New York, N.Y. 10006

   2.____

3. Helen Steam
   5 Metropolitan Oval
   Bronx, N.Y. 10462

   Helene Stearn
   5 Metropolitan Oval
   Bronx, N.Y. 10462

   3.____

4. Jacob Weisman
   231 Francis Lewis Boulevard
   Forest Hills, N.Y. 11325

   Jacob Weisman
   231 Francis Lewis Boulevard
   Forest Hills, N.Y. 11325

   4.____

5. Riccardo Fuente
   134 West 83 Street
   New York, N.Y. 10024

   Riccardo Fuentes
   134 West 88 Street
   New York, N.Y. 10024

   5.____

6. Dennis Lauber
   52 Avenue D
   Brooklyn, N.Y. 11216

   Dennis Lauder
   52 Avenue D
   Brooklyn, N.Y. 11216

   6.____

7. Paul Cutter
   195 Galloway Avenue
   Staten Island, N.Y. 10356

   Paul Cutter
   175 Galloway Avenue
   Staten Island, N.Y. 10365

   7.____

8. Sean Donnelly
   45-58 41 Avenue
   Woodside, N.Y. 11168

   Sean Donnelly
   45-58 41 Avenue
   Woodside, N.Y. 11168

   8.____

9. Clyde Willot
   1483 Rockaway Avenue
   Brooklyn, N.Y. 11238

   Clyde Willat
   1483 Rockaway Avenue
   Brooklyn, N.Y. 11238

   9.____

2 (#4)

COLUMN I	COLUMN II	
10. Michael Stanakis 419 Sheriden Avenue Staten Island, N.Y. 10363	Michael Stanakis 419 Sheraden Avenue Staten Island, N.Y. 10363	10.____
11. Joseph DiSilva 63-84 Saunders Road Rego Park, N.Y. 11431	Joseph Disilva 64-83 Saunders Road Rego Park, N.Y. 11431	11.____
12. Linda Polansky 2224 Fendon Avenue Bronx, N.Y. 20464	Linda Polansky 2255 Fenton Avenue Bronx, N.Y. 10464	12.____
13. Alfred Klein 260 Hillside Terrace Staten Island, N.Y. 15545	Alfred Klein 260 Hillside Terrace Staten Island, N.Y. 15545	13.____
14. William McDonnell 504 E. 55 Street New York, N.Y. 10103	William McConnell 504 E. 55 Street New York, N.Y. 10108	14.____
15. Angela Cipolla 41-11 Parson Avenue Flushing, N.Y. 11446	Angela Cipola 41-11 Parsons Avenue Flushing, N.Y. 11446	15.____
16. Julie Sheridan 1212 Ocean Avenue Brooklyn, N.Y. 11237	Julia Sheridan 1212 Ocean Avenue Brooklyn, N.Y. 11237	16.____
17. Arturo Rodriguez 2156 Cruger Avenue Bronx, N.Y. 10446	Arturo Rodrigues 2156 Cruger Avenue Bronx, N.Y. 10446	17.____
18. Helen McCabe 2044 East 19 Street Brooklyn, N.Y. 11204	Helen McCabe 2040 East 19 Street Brooklyn, N.Y. 11204	18.____
19. Charles Martin 526 West 160 Street New York, N.Y. 10022	Charles Martin 526 West 160 Street New York, N.Y. 10022	19.____
20. Morris Rabinowitz 31 Avenue M Brooklyn, N.Y. 11216	Morris Rabinowitz 31 Avenue N Brooklyn, N.Y. 11216	20.____

KEY (CORRECT ANSWERS)

1.	D	11.	B
2.	B	12.	D
3.	C	13.	A
4.	A	14.	B
5.	B	15.	B
6.	C	16.	C
7.	D	17.	C
8.	A	18.	D
9.	B	19.	A
10.	D	20.	D

TEST 5

DIRECTIONS: In copying the addresses below from Column A to the same line in Column B, an Agent-in-Training made some errors. For Questions 1 through 5, if you find that the agent made an error in
only one line, mark your answer A;
only two lines, mark your answer B;
only three lines, mark your answer C;
all four lines, mark your answer D.

EXAMPLE

COLUMN A	COLUMN B
24 Third Avenue	24 Third Avenue
5 Lincoln Road	5 Lincoln Street
50 Central Park West	6 Central Park West
37-21 Queens Boulevard	21-37 Queens Boulevard

Since errors were made on only three lines, namely the second, third, and fourth, the CORRECT answer is C.
PRINT THE LETTER OF THE CORRECT ANSWER IN THE SPACE AT THE RIGHT.

COLUMN A   COLUMN B

1. 57-22 Springfield Boulevard   75-22 Springfield Boulevard   1.____
   94 Gun Hill Road   94 Gun Hill Avenue
   8 New Dorp Lane   8 New Drop Lane
   36 Bedford Avenue   36 Bedford Avenue

2. 538 Castle Hill Avenue   538 Castle Hill Avenue   2.____
   54-15 Beach Channel Drive   54-15 Beach Channel Drive
   21 Ralph Avenue   21 Ralph Avenue
   162 Madison Avenue   162 Morrison Avenue

3. 49 Thomas Street   49 Thomas Street   3.____
   27-21 Northern Blvd.   21-27 Northern Blvd.
   86 125th Street   86 125th Street
   872 Atlantic Ave.   872 Baltic Ave,

4. 261-17 Horace Harding Expwy.   261-17 Horace Harding Pkwy.   4.____
   191 Fordham Road   191 Fordham Road
   6 Victory Blvd.   6 Victoria Blvd.
   552 Oceanic Ave.   552 Ocean Ave.

5. 90-05 38th Avenue   90-05 36th Avenue   5.____
   19 Central Park West   19 Central Park East
   9281 Avenue X   9281 Avenue X
   22 West Farms Square   22 West Farms Square

152

KEY (CORRECT ANSWERS)

1. C
2. A
3. B
4. C
5. B

TEST 6

DIRECTIONS: For Questions 1 through 10, choose the letter in Column II next to the number which EXACTLY matches the number in Column I. *PRINT THE LETTER OF THE CORRECT ANSWER IN THE SPACE AT THE RIGHT.*

<u>COLUMN I</u>   <u>COLUMN II</u>

1. 14235
   A. 13254
   B. 12435
   C. 13245
   D. 14235

   1.____

2. 70698
   A. 90768
   B. 60978
   C. 70698]
   D. 70968

   2.____

3. 11698
   A. 11689
   B. 11986
   C. 11968
   D. 11698

   3.____

4. 50497
   A. 50947
   B. 50497
   C. 50749
   D. 54097

   4.____

5. 69635
   A. 60653
   B. 69630
   C. 69365
   D. 69635

   5.____

6. 1201022011
   A. 1201022011
   B. 1201020211
   C. 1202012011
   D. 1021202011

   6.____

7. 3893981389
   A. 3893891389
   B. 3983981389
   C. 3983891389
   D. 3893981389

   7.____

8. 4765476589
   A. 4765476598
   B. 4765476588
   C. 4765476589
   D. 4765746589

   8.____

9. 8679678938   A. 8679687938   9.____
                         B. 8679678938
                         C. 8697678938
                         D. 8678678938

10. 6834836932   A. 6834386932   10.____
                         B. 6834836923
                         C. 6843836932
                         D. 6834836932

Questions 11-15.

DIRECTIONS: For Questions 11 through 15, determine how many of the symbols in Column Z are exactly the same as the symbol in Column Y.
If none is exactly the same, answer A;
If only one symbol is exactly the same, answer B;
If two symbols are exactly the same, answer C;
If three symbols are exactly the same, answer D.

COLUMN Y | COLUMN Z

11. A123B1266
    A123B1366
    A123B1266
    A133B1366
    A123B1266   11.____

12. CC28D3377
    CD22D3377
    CC38D3377
    CC28C3377
    CC28D2277   12.____

13. M21AB201X
    M12AB201X
    M21AB201X
    M21AB201Y
    M21BA201X   13.____

14. PA383Y744
    AP383Y744
    PA338Y744
    PA388Y744
    PA383Y774   14.____

15. PB2Y8893
    PB2Y8893
    PB2Y8893
    PB3Y8898
    PB2Y8893   15.____

KEY (CORRECT ANSWERS)

1.	D	6.	A	11.	C
2.	C	7.	D	12.	A
3.	D	8.	C	13.	B
4.	B	9.	B	14.	A
5.	D	10.	D	15.	D

EXAMINATION SECTION
TEST 1

DIRECTIONS: In each of the following questions, only one of the four sentences conforms to standards of correct usage. The other three contain errors in grammar, diction, or punctuation. Select the choice in each question which BEST conforms to standards of correct usage. Consider a choice correct if it contains none of the errors mentioned above, even though there may be other ways of expressing the same thought. *PRINT THE LETTER OF THE CORRECT ANSWER IN THE SPACE AT THE RIGHT.*

1. A. Because he was ill was no excuse for his behavior
    B. In insist that he see a lawyer before he goes to trial.
    C. He said "that he had not intended to go."
    D. He wasn't out of the office only three days.

    1.____

2. A. He came to the station and pays a porter to carry his bags into the train.
    B. I should have liked to live in medieval times.
    C. My father was born in Linville. A little country town where everybody knows everyone else.
    D. The car, which is parked across the street, is disabled.

    2.____

3. A. He asked the desk clerk for a clean, quiet, room.
    B. I expected James to be lonesome and that he would want to go home.
    C. I have stopped worrying because I have heard nothing further on the subject.
    D. If the board of directors controls the company, they may take actions which are disapproved by the stockholders.

    3.____

4. A. Each of the players knew their place.
    B. He whom you saw on the stage is the son of an actor.
    C. Susan is the smartest of the twin sisters.
    D. Who ever thought of him winning both prizes?

    4.____

5. A. An outstanding trait of early man was their reliance on omens.
    B. Because I had never been there before.
    C. Neither Mr. Jones nor Mr. Smith has completed his work.
    D. While eating my dinner, a dog came to the window.

    5.____

6. A. A copy of the lease, in addition to the Rules and Regulations, are to be given to each tenant.
    B. The Rules and Regulations and a copy of the lease is being given to each tenant.
    C. A copy of the lease, in addition to the Rules and Regulations, is to be given to each tenant.
    D. A copy of the lease, in addition to the Rules and Regulations, are being given to each tenant.

    6.____

7. A. Although we understood that for him music was a passion, we were disturbed   7._____
       by the fact that he was addicted to sing along with the soloists.
    B. Do you believe that Steven is liable to win a scholarship?
    C. Give the picture to whomever is a connoisseur of art.
    D. Whom do you believe to be the most efficient worker in the office?

8. A. Each adult who is sure they know all the answers will some day realize   8._____
       their mistake.
    B. Even the most hardhearted villain would have to feel bad about so horrible
       a tragedy.
    C. Neither being licensed teachers, both aspirants had to pass rigorous tests
       before being appointed.
    D. The principal reason why he wanted to be designated was because he had
       never before been to a convention.

9. A. Being that the weather was so inclement, the party has been postponed for   9._____
       at least a month.
    B. He is in New York City only three weeks and he has already seen all the
       thrilling sights in Manhattan and in the other four boroughs.
    C. If you will look it up in the official directory, which can be consulted in the
       library during specified hours, you will discover that the chairman and
       director are Mr. T. Henry Long.
    D. Working hard at college during the day and at the post office during the
       night, he appeared to his family to be indefatigable.

10. A. I would have been happy to oblige you if you only asked me to do it.   10._____
    B. The cold weather, as well as the unceasing wind and rain, have made us
       decide to spend the winter in Florida.
    C. The politician would have been more successful in winning office if he
       would have been less dogmatic.
    D. These trousers are expensive; however, they will wear well.

11. A. All except him wore formal attire at the reception for the ambassador.   11._____
    B. If that chair were to be blown off of the balcony, it might injure someone
       below.
    C. Not a passenger, who was in the crash, survived the impact.
    D. To borrow money off friends is the best way to lose them.

12. A. Approaching Manhattan on the ferry boat from Staten Island, an   12._____
       unforgettable sight of the skyscrapers is seen.
    B. Did you see the exhibit of modernistic paintings as yet?
    C. Gesticulating wildly and ranting in stentorian tones, the speaker was the
       sinecure of all eyes.
    D. The airplane with crew and passengers was lost somewhere in the Pacific
       Ocean.

3 (#1)

13. A. If one has consistently had that kind of training, it is certainly too late to change your entire method of swimming long distances.
    B. The captain would have been more impressed if you would have been more conscientious in evacuation drills.
    C. The passengers on the stricken ship were all ready to abandon it at the signal.
    D. The villainous shark lashed at the lifeboat with it's tail, trying to upset the rocking boat in order to partake of it's contents.

13.____

14. A. As one whose been certified as a professional engineer, I believe that the decision to build a bridge over that harbor is unsound.
    B. Between you and me, this project ought to be completed long before winter arrives.
    C. He fervently hoped that the men would be back at camp and to find them busy at their usual chores.
    D. Much to his surprise, he discovered that the climate of Korea was like his home town.

14.____

15. A. An industrious executive is aided, not impeded, by having a hobby which gives him a fresh point of view on life and its problems.
    B. Frequent absence during the calendar year will surely mitigate against the chances of promotion.
    C. He was unable to go to the committee meeting because he was very ill.
    D. Mr. Brown expressed his disapproval so emphatically that his associates were embarassed

15.____

16. A. At our next session, the office manager will have told you something about his duties and responsibilities.
    B. In general, the book is absorbing and original and have no hesitation about recommending it.
    C. The procedures followed by private industry in dealing with lateness and absence are different from ours.
    D. We shall treat confidentially any information about Mr. Doe, to whom we understand you have sent reports to for many years.

16.____

17. A. I talked to one official, whom I knew was fully impartial.
    B. Everyone signed the petition but him.
    C. He proved not only to be a good student but also a good athlete.
    D. All are incorrect.

17.____

18. A. Every year a large amount of tenants are admitted to housing projects.
    B. Henry Ford owned around a billion dollars in industrial equipment.
    C. He was aggravated by the child's poor behavior.
    D. All are incorrect.

18.____

19. A. Before he was committed to the asylum he suffered from the illusion that he was Napoleon.
    B. Besides stocks, there were also bonds in the safe.
    C. We bet the other team easily.
    D. All are incorrect.

19.____

20. A. Bring this report to your supervisory.
    B. He set the chair down near the table.
    C. The capitol of New York is Albany.
    D. All are incorrect.

20.____

21. A. He was chosen to arbitrate the dispute because everyone knew he would be disinterested.
    B. It is advisable to obtain the best council before making an important decision.
    C. Less college students are interested in teaching than ever before.
    D. All are incorrect.

21.____

22. A. She, hearing a signal, the source lamp flashed.
    B. While hearing a signal, the source lamp flashed.
    C. In hearing a signal, the source lamp flashed.
    D. As she heard a signal, the source lamp flashed.

22.____

23. A. Every one of the time records have been initialed in the designated spaces.
    B. All of the time records has been initialed in the designated spaces.
    C. Each one of the time records was initialed in the designated spaces.
    D. The time records all been initialed in the designated spaces.

23.____

24. A. If there is no one else to answer the phone, you will have to answer it.
    B. You will have to answer it yourself if no one else answers the phone.
    C. If no one else is not around to pick up the phone, you will have to do it.
    D. You will have to answer the phone when nobodys here to do it.

24.____

25. A. Dr. Barnes not in his office. What could I do for you?
    B. Dr. Barnes is not in his office. Is there something I can do for you?
    C. Since Dr. Barnes is not in his office, might there be something I may do for you?
    D. Is there any ways I can assist you since Dr. Barnes is not in his office?

25.____

26. A. She do not understand how the new console works.
    B. The way the new console works, she doesn't understand.
    C. She doesn't understand how the new console works.
    D. The new console works, so that she doesn't understand.

26.____

27. A. Certain changes in my family income must be reported as they occur.
    B. When certain changes in family income occur, it must be reported.
    C. Certain family income change must be reported as they occur.
    D. Certain changes in family income must be reported as they have been occurring.

27.____

28. A. Each tenant has to complete the application themselves.
     B. Each of the tenants have to complete the application by himself.
     C. Each of the tenants has to complete the application himself.
     D. Each of the tenants has to complete the application by themselves.

     28.____

29. A. Yours is the only building that the construction will effect.
     B. Your's is the only building affected by the construction.
     C. The construction will only effect your building.
     D. Yours is the only building that will be affected by the construction.

     29.____

30. A. There is four tests left.
     B. The number of tests left are four.
     C. There are four tests left.
     D. Four of the tests remains.

     30.____

31. A. Each of the applicants takes a test.
     B. Each of the applicant take a test.
     C. Each of the applicants take tests.
     D. Each of the applicants have taken tests.

     31.____

32. A. The applicant, not the examiners, are ready.
     B. The applicants, not the examiners, is ready.
     C. The applicants, not the examiner, are ready.
     D. The applicant, not the examiner, are ready

     32.____

33. A. You will not progress except you practice.
     B. You will not progress without you practicing.
     C. You will not progress unless you practice.
     D. You will not progress provided you do not practice.

     33.____

34. A. Neither the director or the employees will be at the office tomorrow.
     B. Neither the director nor the employees will be at the office tomorrow.
     C. Neither the director, or the secretary nor the other employees will be at the office tomorrow.
     D. Neither the director, the secretary or the other employees will be at the office tomorrow.

     34.____

35. A. In my absence, he and her will have to finish the assignment.
     B. In my absence he and she will have to finish the assignment.
     C. In my absence she and him, they will have to finish the assignment.
     D. In my absence he and her both will have to finish the assignment.

     35.____

KEY (CORRECT ANSWERS)

1.	B	11.	A	21.	A	31.	A
2.	B	12.	D	22.	D	32.	C
3.	C	13.	C	23.	C	33.	C
4.	B	14.	B	24.	A	34.	B
5.	C	15.	A	25.	B	35.	B
6.	C	16.	C	26.	C		
7.	D	17.	B	27.	A		
8.	B	18.	D	28.	C		
9.	D	19.	B	29.	D		
10.	D	20.	B	30.	C		

TEST 2

DIRECTIONS: Each question or incomplete statement is followed by several suggested answers or completions. Select the one that BEST answers the question or completes the statement. *PRINT THE LETTER OF THE CORRECT ANSWER IN THE SPACE AT THE RIGHT.*

Questions 1-4.

DIRECTIONS: Questions 1 through 4 consist of three sentences each. For each question, select the sentence which contains NO error in grammar or usage.

1. A. Be sure that everybody brings his notes to the conference.
   B. He looked like he meant to hit the boy.
   C. Mr. Jones is one of the clients who was chosen to represent the district.
   D. All are incorrect.

   1.____

2. A. He is taller than I.
   B. I'll have nothing to do with these kind of people.
   C. The reason why he will not buy the house is because it is too expensive.
   D. All are incorrect.

   2.____

3. A. Aren't I eligible for this apartment.
   B. Have you seen him anywheres?
   C. He should of come earlier.
   D. All are incorrect.

   3.____

4. A. He graduated college in 1982.
   B. He hadn't but one more line to write.
   C. Who do you think is the author of this report?
   D. All are incorrect.

   4.____

Questions 5-35.

DIRECTIONS: In each of the following questions, only one of the four sentences conforms to standards of correct usage. The other three contain errors in grammar, diction, or punctuation. Select the choice in each question which BEST conforms to standards of correct usage. Consider a choice correct if it contains none of the errors mentioned above, even though there may be other ways of expressing the same thought.

5. A. It is obvious that no one wants to be a kill-joy if they can help it.
   B. It is not always possible, and perhaps it never ispossible, to judge a person's character by just looking at him.
   C. When Yogi Berra of the New York Yankees hit an immortal grandslam home run, everybody in the huge stadium including Pittsburgh fans, rose to his feet.
   D. Every one of us students must pay tuition today.

   5.____

6. A. The physician told the young mother that if the baby is not able to digest its milk, it should be boiled.
    B. There is no doubt whatsoever that he felt deeply hurt because John Smith had betrayed the trust.
    C. Having partaken of a most delicious repast prepared by Tessie Breen, the hostess, the horses were driven home immediately thereafter.
    D. The attorney asked my wife and myself several questions.

6._____

7. A. Despite all denials, there is no doubt in my mind that
    B. At this time everyone must deprecate the demogogic attack made by one of our Senators on one of our most revered statesmen.
    C. In the first game of a crucial two-game series, Ted Williams, got two singles, both of them driving in a run.
    D. Our visitor brought good news to John and I.

7._____

8. A. If he would have told me, I should have been glad to help him in his dire financial emergency.
    B. Newspaper men have often asserted that diplomats or so-called official spokesmen sometimes employ equivocation in attempts to deceive.
    C. I think someones coming to collect money for the Red Cross.
    D. In a masterly summation, the young attorney expressed his belief that the facts clearly militate against this opinion.

8._____

9. A. We have seen most all the exhibits.
    B. Without in the least underestimating your advice, in my opinion the situation has grown immeasurably worse in the past few days.
    C. I wrote to the box office treasurer of the hit show that a pair of orchestra seats would be preferable.
    D. As the grim story of Pearl Harbor was broadcast on that fateful December 7, it was the general opinion that war was inevitable.

9._____

10. A. Without a moment's hesitation, Casey Stengel said that Larry Berra works harder than any player on the team.
    B. There is ample evidence to indicate that many animals can run faster than any human being.
    C. No one saw the accident but I.
    D. Example of courage is the heroic defense put up by the paratroopers against overwhelming odds.

10._____

11. A. If you prefer these kind, Mrs. Grey, we shall be more than willing to let you have them reasonably.
    B. If you like these here, Mrs. Grey, we shall be more than willing to let you have them reasonably.
    C. If you like these, Mrs. Grey, we shall be more than willing to let you have them.
    D. Who shall we appoint?

11._____

12. A. The number of errors are greater in speech than in writing. 12._____
    B. The doctor rather than the nurse was to blame for his being neglected.
    C. Because the demand for these books have been so great, we reduced the price.
    D. John Galsworthy, the English novelist, could not have survived a serious illness; had it not been for loving care.

13. A. Our activities this year have seldom ever been as interesting as they have been this month. 13._____
    B. Our activities this month have been more interesting, or at least as interesting as those of any month this year.
    C. Our activities this month has been more interesting than those of any other month this year.
    D. Neither Jean nor her sister was at home.

14. A. George B. Shaw's view of common morality, as well as his wit sparkling with a dash of perverse humor here and there, have led critics to term him "The Incurable Rebel." 14._____
    B. The President's program was not always received with the wholehearted endorsement of his own party, which is why the party faces difficulty in drawing up a platform for the coming election.
    C. The reason why they wanted to travel was because they had never been away from home.
    D. Facing a barrage of cameras, the visiting celebrity found it extremely difficult to express his opinions clearly.

15. A. When we calmed down, we all agreed that our anger had been kind of unnecessary and had not helped the situation. 15._____
    B. Without him going into all the details, he made us realize the horror of the accident.
    C. Like one girl, for example, who applied for two positions.
    D. Do not think that you have to be so talented as he is in order to play in the school orchestra.

16. A. He looked very peculiarly to me. 16._____
    B. He certainly looked at me peculiar.
    C. Due to the train's being late, we had to wait an hour.
    D. The reason for the poor attendance is that it is raining.

17. A. About one out of four own an automobile. 17._____
    B. The collapse of the old Mitchell Bridge was caused by defective construction in the central pier.
    C. Brooks Atkinson was well acquainted with the best literature, thus helping him to become an able critic.
    D. He has to stand still until the relief man comes up, thus giving him no chance to move about and keep warm.

18. A. He is sensitive to confusion and withdraws from people whom he feels are too noisy.
    B. Do you know whether the data is statistically correct?
    C. Neither the mayor or the aldermen are to blame.
    D. Of those who were graduated from high school, a goodly percentage went to college.

19. A. Acting on orders, the offices were searched by a designated committee.
    B. The answer probably is nothing.
    C. I thought it to be all right to excuse them from class.
    D. I think that he is as successful a singer, if not more successful, than Mary.

20. A. $120,000 is really very little to pay for such a wellbuilt house.
    B. The creatures looked like they had come from outer space.
    C. It was her, he knew!
    D. Nobody but me knows what to do.

21. A. Mrs. Smith looked good in her new suit.
    B. New York may be compared with Chicago.
    C. I will not go to the meeting except you go with me.
    D. I agree with this editorial.

22. A. My opinions are different from his.
    B. There will be less students in class now.
    C. Helen was real glad to find her watch.
    D. It had been pushed off of her dresser.

23. A. Almost everyone, who has been to California, returns with glowing reports.
    B. George Washington, John Adams, and Thomas Jefferson, were our first presidents.
    C. Mr. Walters, whom we met at the bank yesterday, is the man, who gave me my first job.
    D. One should study his lessons as carefully as he can.

24. A. We had such a good time yesterday.
    B. When the bell rang, the boys and girls went in the schoolhouse.
    C. John had the worst headache when he got up this morning.
    D. Today's assignment is somewhat longer than yesterday's.

25. A. Neither the mayor nor the city clerk are willing to talk.
    B. Neither the mayor nor the city clerk is willing to talk.
    C. Neither the mayor or the city clerk are willing to talk.
    D Neither the mayor or the city clerk is willing to talk.

26. A. Being that he is that kind of boy, cooperation cannot be expected.
    B. He interviewed people who he thought had something to say.
    C. Stop whomever enters the building regardless of rank or office held.
    D. Passing through the countryside, the scenery pleased us.

5 (#2)

27. A. The childrens' shoes were in their closet.   27.____
    B. The children's shoes were in their closet.
    C. The childs' shoes were in their closet.
    D. The childs' shoes were in his closet.

28. A. An agreement was reached between the defendant, the plaintiff, the   28.____
       plaintiff's attorney and the insurance company as to the amount of the
       settlement.
    B. Everybody was asked to give their versions of the accident.
    C. The consensus of opinion was that the evidence was inconclusive.
    D. The witness stated that if he was rich, he wouldn't have had to loan the
       money.

29. A. Before beginning the investigation, all the materials related to the case were   29.____
       carefully assembled.
    B. The reason for his inability to keep the appointment is because of his injury
       in the accident.
    C. This here evidence tends to support the claim of the defendant.
    D. We interviewed all the witnesses who, according to the driver, were still in
       town.

30. A. Each claimant was allowed the full amount of their medical expenses.   30.____
    B. Either of the three witnesses is available.
    C. Every one of the witnesses was asked to tell his story.
    D. Neither of the witnesses are right.

31. A. The commissioner, as well as his deputy and various bureau heads, were   31.____
       present.
    B. A new organization of employers and employees have been formed.
    C. One or the other of these men have been selected.
    D. The number of pages in the book is enough to discourage a reader.

32. A. Between you and me, I think he is the better man.   32.____
    B. He was believed to be me.
    C. Is it us that you wish to see?
    D. The winners are him and her.

33. A. Beside the statement to the police, the witness spoke to no one.   33.____
    B. He made no statement other than to the police and I.
    C. He made no statement to any one else, aside from the police.
    D. The witness spoke to no one but me.

34. A. The claimant has no one to blame but himself.   34.____
    B. The boss sent us, he and I, to deliver the packages.
    C. The lights come from mine and not his car.
    D. There was room on the stairs for him and myself.

35. A. Admission to this clinic is limited to patients' inability to pay for medical care.
     B. Patients who can pay little or nothing for medical care are treated in this clinic.
     C. The patient's ability to pay for medical care is the determining factor in his admission to this clinic.
     D. This clinic is for the patient's that cannot afford to pay or that can pay a little for medical care.

35.____

KEY (CORRECT ANSWERS)

1. A	11. C	21. A	31. D
2. A	12. B	22. A	32. A
3. D	13. D	23. D	33. D
4. C	14. D	24. D	34. A
5. D	15. D	25. B	35. B
6. D	16. D	26. B	
7. B	17. B	27. B	
8. B	18. D	28. C	
9. D	19. B	29. D	
10. B	20. D	30. C	

PREPARING WRITTEN MATERIAL
EXAMINATION SECTION
TEST 1

DIRECTIONS: Each of the sentences in this test may be classified under one of the following four categories:
  A. *Incorrect* because of faulty grammar or sentence structure
  B. *Incorrect* because of faulty punctuation
  C. *Incorrect* because of faulty capitalization
  D. *Correct*

Examine each sentence carefully to determine under which of the above four options it is best classified. Then, in the space at the right, print the capital letter preceding the option which is the BEST of the four suggested above.

(Each incorrect sentence contains but one type of error. Consider a sentence to be correct if it contains none of the types of errors mentioned, even though there may be other correct ways of expressing the same thought.)

1. This fact, together with those brought out at the previous meeting, prove that the schedule is satisfactory to the employees.   1.____

2. Like many employees in scientific fields, the work of bookkeepers and accountants requires accuracy and neatness.   2.____

3. "What can I do for you," the secretary asked as she motioned to the visitor to take a seat.   3.____

4. Our representative, Mr. Charles will call on you next week to determine whether or not your claim has merit.   4.____

5. We expect you to return in the spring; please do not disappoint us.   5.____

6. Any supervisor, who disregards the just complaints of his subordinates, is remiss in the performance of his duty.   6.____

7. Because she took less than an hour for lunch is no reason for permitting her to leave before five o'clock.   7.____

8. "Miss Smith," said the supervisor, "Please arrange a meeting of the staff for two o'clock on Monday."   8.____

9. A private company's vacation and sick leave allowance usually differs considerably from a public agency.   9.____

10. Therefore, in order to increase the efficiency of operations in the department, a report on the recommended changes in procedures was presented to the departmental committee in charge of the program.   10.____

11. We told him to assign the work to whoever was available. 11.____

12. Since John was the most efficient of any other employee in the bureau, he received the highest service rating. 12.____

13. Only those members of the national organization who resided in the middle West attended the conference in Chicago. 13.____

14. The question of whether the office manager has as yet attained, or indeed can ever hope to secure professional status is one which has been discussed for years. 14.____

15. No one knew who to blame for the error which, we later discovered, resulted in a considerable loss of time. 15.____

KEY (CORRECT ANSWERS)

1.	A	6.	B	11.	D
2.	A	7.	A	12.	A
3.	B	8.	C	13.	C
4.	B	9.	A	14.	B
5.	D	10.	D	15.	A

TEST 2

DIRECTIONS: Each of the sentences in this test may be classified under one of the following four categories:
- A. *Incorrect* because of faulty grammar or sentence structure
- B. *Incorrect* because of faulty punctuation
- C. *Incorrect* because of faulty capitalization
- D. *Correct*

1. The National alliance of Businessmen is trying to persuade private businesses to hire youth in the summertime. 1.____

2. The supervisor who is on vacation, is in charge of processing vouchers. 2.____

3. The activity of the committee at its conferences is always stimulating. 3.____

4. After checking the addresses again, the letters went to the mailroom. 4.____

5. The director, as well as the employees, are interested in sharing the dividends. 5.____

KEY (CORRECT ANSWERS)

1. C
2. B
3. D
4. A
5. A

TEST 3

DIRECTIONS: In each of the following groups of sentences, one of the four sentences is faulty in grammar, punctuation, or capitalization. Select the INCORRECT sentence in each case.

1. A. Sailing down the bay was a thrilling experience for me.
   B. He was not consulted about your joining the club.
   C. This story is different than the one I told you yesterday.
   D. There is no doubt about his being the best player.

   1._____

2. A. He maintains there is but one road to world peace.
   B. It is common knowledge that a child sees much he is not supposed to see.
   C. Much of the bitterness might have been avoided if arbitration had been resorted to earlier in the meeting.
   D. The man decided it would be advisable to marry a girl somewhat younger than him.

   2._____

3. A. In this book, the incident I liked least is where the hero tries to put out the forest fire.
   B. Learning a foreign language will undoubtedly give a person a better understanding of his mother tongue.
   C. His actions made us wonder what he planned to do next.
   D. Because of the war, we were unable to travel during the summer vacation.

   3._____

4. A. The class had no sooner become interested in the lesson than the dismissal bell rang.
   B. There is little agreement about the kind of world to be planned at the peace conference.
   C. "Today," said the teacher, "we shall read 'The Wind in the Willows,' I am sure you'll like it.
   D. The terms of the legal settlement of the family quarrel handicapped both sides for many years.

   4._____

5. A. I was so surprised that I was not able to say a word.
   B. She is taller than any other member of the class.
   C. It would be much more preferable if you were never seen in his company.
   D. We had no choice but to excuse her for being late.

   5._____

KEY (CORRECT ANSWERS)

1. C
2. D
3. A
4. C
5. C

TEST 4

DIRECTIONS: In each of the following groups of sentences, one of the four sentences is faulty in grammar, punctuation, or capitalization. Select the INCORRECT sentence in each case.

1. A. Please send me these data at the earliest opportunity.
   B. The loss of their material proved to be a severe handicap.
   C. My principal objection to this plan is that it is impracticable.
   D. The doll had laid in the rain for an hour and was ruined.

   1._____

2. A. The garden scissors, left out all night in the rain, were in a badly rusted condition.
   B. The girls felt bad about the misunderstanding which had arisen
   C. Sitting near the campfire, the old man told John and I about many exciting adventures he had had.
   D. Neither of us is in a position to undertake a task of that magnitude.

   2._____

3. A. The general concluded that one of the three roads would lead to the besieged city.
   B. The children didn't, as a rule, do hardly anything beyond what they were told to do.
   C. The reason the girl gave for her negligence was that she had acted on the spur of the moment.
   D. The daffodils and tulips look beautiful in that blue vase.

   3._____

4. A. If I was ten years older, I should be interested in this work.
   B. Give the prize to whoever has drawn the best picture.
   C. When you have finished reading the book, take it back to the library.
   D. My drawing is as good as or better than yours.

   4._____

5. A. He asked me whether the substance was animal or vegetable.
   B. An apple which is unripe should not be eaten by a child.
   C. That was an insult to me who am your friend.
   D. Some spy must of reported the matter to the enemy.

   5._____

6. A. Limited time makes quoting the entire message impossible.
   B. Who did she say was going?
   C. The girls in your class have dressed more dolls this year than we.
   D. There was such a large amount of books on the floor that I couldn't find a place for my rocking chair.

   6._____

7. A. What with his sleeplessness and his ill health, he was unable to assume any responsibility for the success of the meeting.
   B. If I had been born in February, I should be celebrating my birthday soon.
   C. In order to prevent breakage, she placed a sheet of paper between each of the plates when she packed them.
   D. After the spring shower, the violets smelled very sweet.

   7._____

2 (#4)

8.
   A. He had laid the book down very reluctantly before the end of the lesson.
   B. The dog, I am sorry to say, had lain on the bed all night.
   C. The cloth was first lain on a flat surface; then it was pressed with a hot iron.
   D. While we were in Florida, we lay in the sun until we were noticeably tanned.

   8.____

9.
   A. If John was in New York during the recent holiday season, I have no doubt he spent most of the time with his parents.
   B. How could he enjoy the television program; the dog was barking and the baby was crying.
   C. When the problem was explained to the class, he must have been asleep.
   D. She wished that her new dress were finished so that she could go to the party.

   9.____

10.
    A. The engine not only furnishes power but light and heat as well.
    B. You're aware that we've forgotten whose guilt was established, aren't you?
    C. Everybody knows that the woman made many sacrifices for her children.
    D. A man with his dog and gun is a familiar sight in this neighborhood.

    10.____

KEY (CORRECT ANSWERS)

1.	D	6.	D
2.	C	7.	B
3.	B	8.	C
4.	A	9.	B
5.	D	10.	A

TEST 5

DIRECTIONS: Each of Questions 1 through 5 consists of a sentence which may be classified appropriately under one of the following four categories:
  A. *Incorrect* because of faulty grammar
  B. *Incorrect* because of faulty punctuation
  C. *Incorrect* because of faulty spelling
  D. *Correct*

Examine each sentence carefully. Then, print in the space at the right the letter preceding the category which is the BEST of the four suggested above
(Note: Each incorrect sentence contains only one type of error. Consider a sentence correct if it contains no errors, although there may be other correct ways of writing the sentence.)

1. Of the two employees, the one in our office is the most efficient.   1.____

2. No one can apply or even understand, the new rules and regulations.   2.____

3. A large amount of supplies were stored in the empty office.   3.____

4. If an employee is occassionally asked to work overtime, he should do so willingly.   4.____

5. It is true that the new procedures are difficult to use but, we are certain that you will learn them quickly.   5.____

6. The office manager said that he did not know who would be given a large allotment under the new plan.   6.____

7. It was at the supervisor's request that the clerk agreed to postpone his vacation.   7.____

8. We do not believe that it is necessary for both he and the clerk to attend the conference.   8.____

9. All employees, who display perseverance, will be given adequate recognition.   9.____

10. He regrets that some of us employees are dissatisfied with our new assignments.   10.____

11. "Do you think that the raise was merited," asked the supervisor?   11.____

12. The new manual of procedure is a valuable supplement to our rules and regulations.   12.____

13. The typist admitted that she had attempted to pursuade the other employees to assist her in her work.   13.____

2 (#5)

14. The supervisor asked that all amendments to the regulations be handled by you and I. 14.____

15. The custodian seen the boy who broke the window. 15.____

KEY (CORRECT ANSWERS)

1.	A	6.	D	11.	B
2.	B	7.	D	12.	C
3.	A	8.	A	13.	C
4.	C	9.	B	14.	A
5.	B	10.	D	15.	A

www.ingramcontent.com/pod-product-compliance
Lightning Source LLC
Chambersburg PA
CBHW080732230426
43665CB00020B/2715